D1248683

# Collected Poems
## (1930–1973)

*Books by May Sarton*

POETRY

Encounter in April
Inner Landscape
The Lion and the Rose
The Leaves of the Tree
The Land of Silence
In Time Like Air
Cloud, Stone, Sun, Vine
A Private Mythology
As Does New Hampshire
A Grain of Mustard Seed
A Durable Fire
Collected Poems (1930–1973)

NOVELS

The Single Hound
The Bridge of Years
Shadow of a Man
A Shower of Summer Days
Faithful Are the Wounds
The Birth of a Grandfather
The Fur Person
The Small Room
Joanna and Ulysses
Mrs. Stevens Hears the Mermaids Singing
Miss Pickthorn and Mr. Hare
The Poet and the Donkey
Kinds of Love
As We Are Now

NONFICTION

I Knew a Phoenix
Plant Dreaming Deep
Journal of a Solitude

# Collected Poems

## (1930–1973)

By MAY SARTON

W. W. NORTON & CO., INC., NEW YORK, N. Y.

~

Copyright © 1974 by May Sarton
First Edition
Library of Congress Cataloging in Publication Data
Sarton, May, 1912–
    Collected poems (1930–1973).
PS3537.A832A17    1974        811'.5'2        74-1259
ISBN 0-393-04386-X
1 2 3 4 5 6 7 8 9 0

# Contents

*Encounter in April*    (1930–1937)

| | |
|---|---|
| First Snow | 19 |
| "She Shall Be Called Woman" | 20 |
| Strangers | 27 |

*Inner Landscape*    (1936–1938)

| | |
|---|---|
| Prayer before Work | 31 |
| Architectural Image | 32 |
| Understatement | 33 |
| Summary | 34 |
| Address to the Heart | 35 |
| Memory of Swans | 36 |
| After Silence | 37 |
| Canticle | 38 |
| From Men Who Died Deluded | 39 |
| Afternoon on Washington Street | 40 |
| Winter Evening | 41 |
| A Letter to James Stephens | 42 |

*The Lion and the Rose*    (1938–1948)

| | |
|---|---|
| Monticello | 47 |
| Charleston Plantations | 48 |
| Where the Peacock Cried | 49 |
| In Texas | 50 |
| Boulder Dam | 51 |
| Colorado Mountains | 52 |
| Of the Seasons | 53 |
| Meditation in Sunlight | 54 |
| Difficult Scene | 55 |
| The Window | 56 |
| The Lion and the Rose | 57 |

Indian Dances                                          58
Santos: New Mexico                                     60
Poet in Residence:                                     61
    The Students                                       61
    Campus                                             62
    Before Teaching                                    63
    After Teaching                                     63
    Place of Learning                                  64
The Work of Happiness                                  66
After a Train Journey                                  67
O Who Can Tell?                                        68
The Clavichord                                         69
Song: "Now let us honor with violin and flute"         70
In Memoriam                                            71
Now Voyager                                            73
My Sisters, O My Sisters                               74
The Lady and the Unicorn                               78
Question                                               79
Perspective                                            80
Return                                                 81
"O Saisons! O Châteaux!"                               82
These Pure Arches                                      83
We Have Seen the Wind                                  84
Homage to Flanders                                     85
The Sacred Order                                       86
What the Old Man Said                                  87
Navigator                                              88
Who Wakes                                              89
Return to Chartres                                     90
To the Living                                          91
The Tortured                                           95
The Birthday                                           96

*The Leaves of the Tree*   (1948–1950)
    Myth                                               99
    Song without Music                                100
    The Swans                                         101
    The Second Spring                                 102
    Kot's House                                       103
    To an Honest Friend                               104

# Contents

Landscape Pursued by a Cloud                      105
Evening Music                                     106
Lullaby                                           107
Islands and Wells                                108
Boy by the Waterfall                             109
Poets and the Rain                               110
Winter Grace                                     112

*The Land of Silence*   (1950–1953)
The First Autumn                                 115
The Sacred Wood                                  116
Summer Music                                     117
As Does New Hampshire                           118
Transition                                       119
Villanelle for Fireworks                         120
Provence                                         121
Journey by Train                                 122
Evening in France                                123
From All Our Journeys                            124
Where Warriors Stood                            126
Take Anguish for Companion                       127
Innumerable Friend                               128
The Caged Bird                                   130
The Land of Silence                             131
Letter to an Indian Friend                       132
Of Prayer                                        133
The Tree                                         135
A Light Left On                                  136
Because What I Want Most is Permanence           137
Song: "This is the love I bring"                 138
Leaves before the Wind                           139
In a Dry Land                                    140
Prothalamion                                     141
Kinds of Wind                                    142
The Seas of Wheat                               143
These Images Remain:                             144
    "Now that the evening gathers up the day"    144
    "Even such fervor must seek out an end"      144
    "So to release the soul, search out the soul" 144
    "The rose has opened and is all accomplished" 145

"But parting is return, the coming home"  145
"The stone withstands, but the chisel destroys"  146
"What angel can I leave, gentle and stern"  146
"These images remain, these classic landscapes"  146
"Here are the peaceful days we never knew"  147
Without the Violence  148
Humpty Dumpty  149
Giant in the Garden  150
Journey toward Poetry  151
Italian Garden  152
Letter from Chicago  153
On a Winter Night  155
Now I Become Myself  156

## In Time Like Air   (1953–1958)

A Celebration for George Sarton  159
Dialogue  161
The Furies  162
The Action of the Beautiful  163
On Being Given Time  164
The Metaphysical Garden  165
Where Dream Begins  168
Lament for Toby, a French Poodle  169
Green Song  170
These Were Her Nightly Journeys  171
The Olive Grove  173
Mediterranean  174
At Muzot  175
To the North  176
After Four Years  177
Somersault  179
The Frog, that Naked Creature  180
The Phoenix  181
In Time Like Air  182
Nativity  183
Annunciation  184
All Souls  185
Lifting Stone  186
Binding the Dragon  187
The Fall  188

# Contents

The Other Place                                        189
Definition                                             190
Forethought                                            191
A Pair of Hands                                        192
My Father's Death                                      193
The Light Years                                        194
Spring Day                                             195
By Moonlight                                            196
Reflections in a Double Mirror                         197
Death and the Lovers                                   198

## Cloud, Stone, Sun, Vine   (1958–1961)

A Divorce of Lovers:                                   201
  "Now these two warring halves are to be parted"   201
  "I shall not see the end of this unweaving"       201
  "One death's true death, and that is—not to care" 201
  "Did you achieve this with a simple word"         202
  "What price serenity these cruel days"            202
  "Dear fellow-sufferer, dear cruelty"              203
  "Your greatness withers when it shuts out grief"  203
  "Now we have lost the heartways and the word"     203
  "What if a homing pigeon lost its home"           204
  "So drive back hating Love and loving Hate"        204
  "It does not mean that we shall find the place"    205
  "Others have cherished, perhaps loved me more"     205
  "Wild seas, wild seas, and the gulls veering close" 206
  "For all the loving words and difficult"          206
  "As I look out on the long swell of fields"       206
  "The cat sleeps on my desk in the pale sun"        207
  "After a night of driving rain, the skies"        207
  "These riches burst from every barren tree"        208
  "Where do I go? Nowhere. And who am I"            208
  "Now silence, silence, silence, and within it"    208
Moving In                                              210
Reflections by a Fire                                  211
Mud Season                                             213
Spring Planting                                        214
A Flower-Arranging Summer                              215
Hour of Proof                                          217
Der Abschied                                           218

## A *Private Mythology* (1961–1966)

| | |
|---|---|
| The Beautiful Pauses | 223 |
| A Child's Japan | 224 |
| A Country House | 226 |
| Kyoko | 227 |
| Japanese Prints | 229 |
|    Four Views of Fujiyama | 229 |
|    On the Way to Lake Chuzen-ji | 229 |
|    Lake Chuzen-ji | 229 |
|    Enkaku-ji, Zen Monastery | 230 |
|    Three Variations on a Theme | 230 |
|    Seen from a Train | 230 |
|    The Leopards at Nanzen-ji | 231 |
|    At Katsura, Imperial Villa | 231 |
|    The Inland Sea | 232 |
|    Tourist | 232 |
|    In a Bus | 232 |
|    Carp Garden | 232 |
| A Nobleman's House | 233 |
| Inn at Kyoto | 234 |
| An Exchange of Gifts | 236 |
| The Stone Garden | 238 |
| Wood, Paper, Stone | 240 |
| The Approach—Calcutta | 243 |
| Notes from India | 244 |
|    1. At Bhubaneswar | 244 |
|    2. At Kanarak | 246 |
|    3. At Puri | 247 |
|    4. At Fathpur Sikri | 248 |
| In Kashmir | 249 |
| The Sleeping God | 250 |
| Birthday on the Acropolis | 251 |
| Nostalgia for India | 254 |
| On Patmos | 255 |
| Another Island | 256 |
| At Lindos | 257 |
| At Delphi | 258 |
| Ballads of the Traveler | 260 |
| Lazarus | 263 |

# Contents

"Heureux Qui, Comme Ulysse . . ." 265
Of Havens 266
The House in Winter 267
Still Life in Snowstorm 268
A Fugue of Wings 269
An Observation 271
Learning about Water 272
An Artesian Well 274
A Late Mowing 276
A Country Incident 277
Second Thoughts on the Abstract Gardens of Japan 278
A Village Tale 280
The Horse-Pulling 282
Franz, a Goose 284
Lovers at the Zoo 285
Death and the Turtle 286
Elegy for Meta 287
Death of a Psychiatrist 289
Conversation in Black and White 291
The Walled Garden at Clondalkin 292
A Recognition 295
Joy in Provence 297
Baroque Image 299

## As Does New Hampshire (1967)

Winter Night 303
March-Mad 304
Metamorphosis 305
Apple Tree in May 306
A Glass of Water 307
Stone Walls 308
A Guest 309

## A Grain of Mustard Seed (1967–1971)

A Ballad of the Sixties 313
The Rock in the Snowball 315
The Invocation to Kali 316
    The Kingdom of Kali 316
    The Concentration Camps 317
    The Time of Burning 319

After the Tiger                                          321
"We'll to the Woods No More, the Laurels
   Are Cut Down"                           323
Night Watch                                              324
Proteus                                                  328
A Last Word                                              329
Girl with 'Cello                                         331
The Muse as Medusa                                       332
For Rosalind                                             333
The Great Transparencies                                334
Friendship: The Storms                                   335
Evening Walk in France                                   336
Dutch Interior                                           337
A Vision of Holland                                      338
Bears and Waterfalls                                     339
A Parrot                                                 341
Eine Kleine Snailmusik                                   342
The Fig                                                  343
A Hard Death                                             344
The Silence                                              346
Annunciation                                             347
At Chartres                                              348
Once More at Chartres                                    349
Jonah                                                    350
Easter Morning                                           351
The Godhead as Lynx                                      352
The Waves                                                354
Beyond the Question                                      355
Invocation                                               358

A *Durable Fire*   (1969–1972)

Gestalt at Sixty                                         361
Myself to Me                                             365
Dear Solid Earth                                         366
The Return of Aphrodite                                  367
Inner Space                                              368
Things Seen                                              369
Mozart Again                                             370
The Tree Peony                                           371
A Chinese Landscape                                      372

# Contents 13

| | |
|---|---|
| Reeds and Water | 373 |
| The Snow Light | 374 |
| Warning | 375 |
| Surfers | 376 |
| All Day I Was with Trees | 377 |
| A Storm of Angels | 378 |
| The Angels and the Furies | 379 |
| After an Island | 381 |
| Fulfillment | 384 |
| The Autumn Sonnets: | 385 |
|   "Under the leaves an infant love lies dead" | 385 |
|   "If I can let you go as trees let go" | 385 |
|   "I wake to gentle mist over the meadow" | 385 |
|   "I never thought that it could be, not once" | 386 |
|   "After a night of rain the brilliant screen" | 386 |
|   "As if the house were dying or already dead" | 387 |
|   "Twice I have set my heart upon a sharing" | 387 |
|   "I ponder it again and know for sure" | 387 |
|   "This was our testing year after the first" | 388 |
|   "We watched the waterfalls, rich and baroque" | 388 |
|   "For steadfast flame wood must be seasoned" | 389 |
| February Days | 390 |
| Note to a Photographer | 391 |
| March in New England | 392 |
| Composition | 393 |
| Burial | 394 |
| Of Grief | 395 |
| Prisoner at a Desk | 397 |
| Birthday Present | 398 |
| Elegy for Louise Bogan | 399 |
| Letters to a Psychiatrist: | 400 |
|   Christmas Letter, 1970 | 400 |
|   The Fear of Angels | 402 |
|   The Action of Therapy | 403 |
|   I Speak of Change | 408 |
|   Easter 1971 | 409 |
|   The Contemplation of Wisdom | 409 |
| Index | 411 |

# Collected Poems

## (1930–1973)

# Encounter in April
## (1930–1937)

# First Snow

This is the first soft snow
That tiptoes up to your door
As you sit by the fire and sew,
That sifts through a crack in the **floor**
And covers you hair with hoar.

This is the stiffening wound
Burning the heart of a deer
Chased by a moon-white hound,
This is the hunt and the queer
Sick beating of feet that fear.

This is the crisp despair
Lying close to the marrow,
Fallen out of the air
Like frost on the narrow
Bone of a shot sparrow.

This is the love that will seize
Savagely onto your mind
And do whatever he please,
This the despair, and a moon-blind
Hound you will never bind.

# "She Shall Be Called Woman"

*Genesis II, 23*

## 1

She did not cry out
nor move.
She lay quite still
and leaned
against the great curve
of the earth,
and her breast
was like a fruit
bursten of its own sweetness.

She did not move
nor cry out—
she only looked down
at the hand
against her breast.
She looked down
at the naked hand
and wept.

She could not yet endure
this delicate savage
to lie upon her.
She could not yet endure
the blood to beat so there.
She could not cope
with the first ache
of fullness.

She lay quite still
and looked down
at the hand
where blood was locked
and longed to loose the blood
and let it flow
over her breast
like rain.

## 2

Not on the earth
but surely somewhere
between the elements
of air and sea
she lay that night,
no rim of bone to mark
where body clove to body
and no separate flesh,
strangely impenetrable—
O somewhere surely
did she come
to that clear place
where sky and water meet
and lay transparent there,
knowing the wave.

## 3

She bore the wound of desire
and it did not close,
though she had tried
to burn her hand
and turn one pain
into a simpler pain—
yet it did not close.

She had not known
how strong
the body's will,
how intricate
the stirring of its litheness
that lay now
unstrung,
like a bow—
she saw herself
disrupted at the center
and torn.
And she went into the sea
because her core ached
and there was no healing.

### 4

Not in denial, her peace.
For there in the sea
where she had wished
to leave her body
like a little garment,
she saw now
that not by severing this
would finity be ended
and the atom die,
not so the pure abstract
exist alone.
From those vast places
she must come back
into her particle.
She must put on again
the little garment
of hunger.
Not in denial
her appeasement,
not yet.


### 5

For a long time
it would be pain
and weakness,
and she who worshiped
all straight things
and the narrow breast
would lie relaxed
like an animal asleep,
without strength.

For a long time
a consciousness possessed her
that felt into all grief
as if it were a wound
within herself—
a mouse with its tiny shriek

would leave her
drained and spent.

The unanswerable body
seemed
held in an icy pity
for all livingness—
that was itself
initiate.


6

And then one day
all feeling
slipped out from her skin
until no finger's consciousness remained,
no pain—
and she all turned
to earth
like abstract gravity.
She did not know
how she had come
to close her separate lids
nor where she learned
the gesture of her sleeping,
yet something in her slept
most deeply
and something in her
lay like stone
under a folded dress—
she could not tell how long.


7

Her body was a city
where the soul
had lain asleep,
and now she woke.
She was aware
down to extremity
of how herself was charged,

fiber electric,
a hand under her breast
could hear the dynamo.
A hand upon her wrist
could feel the pulse beat.
She felt the atoms stir,
the myriad expand
and stir

She looked at her hand—
the mesh
with its multitude of lines,
the exquisite small hairs,
the veins
finding their way
down to the nails,
the nails themselves
set in so firmly
with half-moons
at their base,
the fine-set bone,
knuckle and sinew,
and she examined
the mysterious legend
upon the palm—
this was her hand,
a present someone had given her.

And she looked at her breasts
that were firm and full,
standing straightly
out from her chest,
and were each a city
mysteriously part
of other cities.
The earth itself
was not more intricate,
more lovely
than these two
cupped in her hands,
heavy in her hands.

Nothing ever was
as wonderful as this.

## 8

She let her hands
go softly down her skin,
the curving rib,
soft belly
and slim thigh.
She let her hands
slip down
as if they held a shift
and she were trying it
for the first time,
a shining supple garment
she would not want to lose:
So did she clothe herself.

## 9

She would not ever be naked
again—
she would not know
that nakedness
that stretches to the brim
and finds no shelter
from the pure terrific
light of space.
The finite self
had gathered
and was born
out of the infinite,
was hers
and whole.
For the first time
she knew what it meant
to be made so
and molded into this shape
of a pear,
this heaviness of curving fruit.

## 10

There were seeds
within her
that burst at intervals
and for a little while
she would come back
to heaviness,
and then before a surging miracle
of blood,
relax,
and reidentify herself,
each time more closely
with the heart of life.
"I am the beginning,
the never-ending,
the perfect tree."
And she would lean
again as once
on the great curve of the earth,
part of its turning,
as distinctly part
of the universe as a star—
as unresistant,
as completely rhythmical.

## Strangers

There have been two strangers
Who met within a wood
And looked once at each other
Where they stood.

And there have been two strangers
Who met among the heather
And did not look at all
But lay down together.

And there have been two strangers
Who met one April day
And looked long at each other,
And went their way.

*Inner Landscape*
(1936–1938)

# Prayer before Work

Great one, austere,
By whose intent the distant star
Holds its course clear,
Now make this spirit soar—
Give it that ease.

Out of the absolute
Abstracted grief, comfortless, mute,
Sound the clear note,
Pure, piercing as the flute:
Give it precision.

Austere, great one,
By whose grace the inalterable song
May still be wrested from
The corrupt lung:
Give it strict form.

## Architectural Image

Whatever find its place now in this edifice
Must be a buttress to the spire's strict arrow,
No arbitrary grace, no facile artifice
Beyond its compass, absolute and narrow.

Structure imponderable in its ascension,
It is the central nerve, the living spine,
Within it there exists a soaring tension,—
Flight, but deriving from the sternest line.

Whatever arches mold to gentle curve,
Whatever flowers are curved into its face,
Are thrown, are carved to decorate and serve
That motion of a finger into space.

All that is builded here is built to bind
The gentle arch, the stone flower of desire
Into the sterner vision of the mind:
The structure of this passion is a spire.

## Understatement

This wind, corruption in the city
(Spirit pent up in an enclosure),
That steals, seductive, without pity,
The heart's composure.

Think of it gusting over a field today,
Setting the cows to lowing with surprise,
Spreading the sweet smell of manure and hay,
Bringing tears to the eyes.

Oh, there are places where this evil wind
Would work a blessed charm,
Where a wild thing like this warm wind
Would do no harm.

## Summary

In the end it is the dark for which all lovers pine.
They cannot bear the light on their transparent faces,
The light on nerves exposed like a design.
They have a great need of sleep in foreign places,
Of another country than the heart and another speech.
In the end it is escape of which all lovers dream
As men in prison dream of a stretch of beach.
When they toss wide-eyed in their beds they may seem
To think of the cruel mouth and the hard breast
But it is simply murder that their hearts conceive,
Grown savage with the need of dark and rest.
They are ever innocent. They are found to believe
That love endures and their pain is infinite
Who have not learned that each single touch they give,
Every kiss, every word they speak holds death in it:
They are committing murder who merely live.

## Address to the Heart

You cannot go back now to that innocence—
the pure pain that enters like a sword
making the bright blood flow
and the slow perfect healing, leaving you whole.
This is a deeper illness,
a poison that has entered every tissue:
Cut off your hand, you will not find it there.
This must be met and conquered in each separate atom,
must be lived out like a slow fever.
No part is mortally afflicted.
Each part will have its convalescence surely,
and yet you will arise from this infection
changed,
as one returns from death.

## Memory of Swans

The memory of swans comes back to you in sleep;
The landscape is a currentless still stream
Where reeds and rushes stand fast-rooted, deep.
And there the marvelous swan, more white than cream,
More warm than snow, moves as if silence loved him,
Where the dark supple waters ripple and enlace
The soft curve of the breast but have not moved him,
Where fluid passion yields to that cold grace.

So swans proceed, a miracle of pomp across your sleep,
The birds of silence, perfect form and balanced motion:
How will you fashion love, how will you wake and keep
The pride, the purity of a great image freed of its emotion?

## After Silence

Permit the eye so long lost in the inward night
Now to rejoice upon the outward forms of light;
Permit the mind return from those dark secret mazes
To rest a moment in these simple praises;
Permit the spirit homecoming from civil war
To poise itself on silence like a quiet star
That for this moment there may be no other will
Than to be silent, than to be absolutely still—
And then permit this human love to bless
Your further journey into solitariness.

## Canticle

We sat smoking at a table by the river
And then suddenly in the silence someone said,
"Look at the sunlight on the apple tree there shiver:
I shall remember that long after I am dead."
Together we all turned to see how the tree shook,
How it sparkled and seemed spun out of green and gold,
And we thought that hour, that light and our long mutual look
Might warm us each someday when we were cold.

And I thought of your face that sweeps over me like light,
Like the sun on the apple making a lovely show,
So one seeing it marveled the other night,
Turned to me saying, "What is it in your heart? You glow."—
Not guessing that on my face he saw the singular
Reflection of your grace like fire on snow—
And loved you there.

## From Men Who Died Deluded

This is the time to speak to those who will come after,
To those who will climb the mountaintops although
The continual clouds have crept down upon us
And we cannot tell any more how far there is to go.

This is the time to set our lips upon great horns and blow
Far down the years a note to reach them when
They are failing on the crest before the end,
To fall on their ears like a sweet hail from men

Who did not reach so far but blessed their march,
From men who died deluded, far below the peak,
The self-destroyed, unwilling, blinded, caught,
Yet who believed, yet who desired to speak—

Dying, to blow a horn for those who would come after,
Despairing, to send up one clear note from the edge of death
And as the victors falter to salute them proudly
With the hope we cherished with our final breath.

This is the time, this dark time, this bewildered
To give our mortal lives that the great peaceful places
May surely be attained by those who, when they falter,
Must be confronted by the living vision on our dead faces.

## Afternoon on Washington Street

Walking on this dark day through the bewildering city
I came to a familiar street where always shabby men
Stand watching will dull eyes too tired for pity
The news' dispatches written up in chalk for them,
And that indifferent watching held me in suspense,
Fastened my eyes to the same writing they had stopped to read:
Here was the world, bitter and full of wrong and without sense;
Here were the men who soon would be chalked up among the
    shabby dead.
And then I glanced down to a sign among the others written
Of one who on this very day, and in defense of Milton, spoke
Against the curse of Eliot and Pound and I was smitten
With fire at the heart's cockle to think of poet's work.
Cromwell, I could have cried out to the startled and the dour,
Cromwell is dead. There is no one to care a penny for those wars,
But Milton lives, Milton is living at this desperate hour—
Milton, keeping the dark night of the spirit full of stars!

## Winter Evening

The evenings are spun glass these winter days;
They stretch out clear above the dusty litter,
They quietly surround with a pale crystal haze,—
But just before the dark these evenings glitter.
Then for one moment under that clear glass
The fragile earth, the trees, all seem to shiver,
While hangs there, still, most beautiful and ominous,
The darkening sky reflected in the river,
While people peer out just before they pull
The comfortable shades and shut themselves away
From all that's ominous and beautiful,
From what they guess the night might have to say.

## A Letter to James Stephens

James, it is snowing here. It is November.
Think of the good day when we talked together,
For it is time to think of it, remember
What the warm wine, warm friendship, summer weather
Raised in our minds now that it is so cold,
Now that we sit alone and half the world apart,
This bitter season when the young grow old
And sit indoors to weigh the fiery heart:
What of it now? What of this personal all,
The little world these hands have tried to fashion
Using a single theme for their material,
Always a human heart, a human passion?
You said "Seek for a sterner stuff than this,
Look out of your closed spaces to the infinite,
Look beyond hunger and the longed-for kiss
To what there is beyond your love and in it,
To the whole heavy earth and all it bears;
Support the sky. Know the path of the planet,
Until you stand alone, a man who stares
His loneliness out of its depth to span it,
Till you can chisel substance out of space.
Forget your love, your little war, your ache;
Forget that haunting so mysterious face
And write for an abstracted beauty's sake.
Contain a large world in a small strict plan,
Your job is to draw out the essence and provide
The word that will endure, comfort, sustain a man.
This is your honor. This should be your pride."
Dear James, pure poet, I see you with that shell
Held to your sensitive abstracted ear,
Hunting the ocean's rumor till you hear it well,
Until you can set down the sound you hear:—
Fixed to a shell like that you made immortal,
This heart listens, this fragile auricle
Holds rumor like your ocean's, is a portal
That sometimes opens to contain the miracle.
If there are miracles we can record
They happen in the places that you curse.

Blessèd the pure in heart and the enduring word
Sings of that love that spins the universe.
My honor (and I cherish it for it is hardly won)
Is to be pure in this: is to believe
That to write down these perishable songs for one,
For one alone, and out of love, is not to grieve
But to build on the quicksand of despair
A house where every man may take his ease,
May come to shelter from the outer air,
A little house where he may find his peace.
Dear James, if this fire seems only the strange
Quick-burning fire of youth unfounded on the arth
Then may it be transformed but never change.
Let Him in whose hands lie death and birth
Preserve its essence like that bush of flame
That stood up in a path, and, fiery-plumed,
Contained the angel who could speak God's name—
The bush that burned and still was not consumed.

# The Lion and the Rose
# (1938–1948)

# Monticello

This legendary house, this dear enchanted tomb,
Once so supremely lived in, and for life designed,
Will none of moldy death nor give it room,
Charged with the presence of a living mind.

Enter, and touch the temper of a lively man.
See, it is spacious, intimate and full of light.
The eye, pleased by detail, is nourished by the plan;
Nothing is here for show, much for delight.

All the joys of invention and of craft and wit,
Are freely granted here, all given rein,
But taut within the classic form and ruled by it,
Elegant, various, magnificent—and plain,

Europe become implacably American!
Yet Mozart could have been as happy here,
As Monroe riding from his farm again,
As well as any silversmith or carpenter—

As well as we, for whom this elegance,
This freedom in a form, this peaceful grace,
Is not our heritage, although it happened once:
We read the future, not the past, upon his face.

## Charleston Plantations

You cannot see them from the road: go far and deep,
Down the long avenues where mosses cover up the leaves,
Across the empty terraced lawns neglected and asleep,
To the still place where no dog barks and no dove grieves,
And a black mirror gives you back your face too white
In pools dyed jet by cypress roots: go deep and far,
Deep into time, far into crumbling spaces and half-light
To where they stand, our Egypt and our Nineveh.
Deep in a deathly stillness stand the planters' houses.

The garlands and the little foxes' faces carved
Upon the mantels look on empty walls and water-stains
And the stairs tremble though so elegantly curved
(Outside are waiting the bright creeping vines),
And as your foot falls in the silences, you guess
Decay has been arrested for a moment in the wall,
But the gray plumes upon the trees in deathly loveliness
Will stir when you have passed, and somewhere a stone fall.
Deep in a deathly stillness stand the planters' houses.

There is no rice now and the world that sprang from it
Like an azalea, brilliant from the swamps, has crumbled.
A single century, it is embalmed as Egypt.
A single century, and all that elegance was humbled—
While we who fired that world and watched it burn
Come every spring to whisper near the tomb,
To stare, a little shaken, where the mosses mourn
And the azaleas and magnolias have not ceased to bloom.
Deep in a deathly stillness stand the planters' houses.

## Where the Peacock Cried

*The Cotton Kings*
*Natchez, Mississippi*

Nothing could match the era's dazzling façade,
The white grace of the pillars in a gloom of trees;
No sword has scarred, no vulgar hand has overlaid
The pure triumphant form of this American Acropolis:
Nothing could match the era's marvelous shell.

But push the heavy door and enter the dark chill
Of empty halls. Listen while you are told,
"The locks are solid silver, floors the old cypress still,
Mantels Italian marble and twenty-carat gold
Gilds the great mirrors"—that reflect the shabby places
In the imported carpet and the tourists' vacant faces.

This was a beauty bought intact, mourning no dream,
Paid for in cash, perhaps, but with no human breath.
It is as brutal, savage as a peacock's scream,
Emblem of luxury and emptiness and death—
Look for the heart within the house, the center of the cult,
Look for the hearth, the household god, the mystery;
You will not find it where all is perfect to a fault,
Buried and cold under the weight of history,
Gone with the swans that swam artificial lakes.
Did they with violent beating of white wings
Vanish—for all wild beauty death forsakes—
To leave the house to die among its things?

Nothing could match the era's dazzling façade,
Nothing more lovely than the white Grecian portico—
Where, if there was a dream, did the dream go?
Where is the life lived here and what it made?
That when you ask, the smug descendants say,
"We lit a thousand candles here for Henry Clay."
The answer is not war that always has intensified
A living dream.
                    But here the peacock cried.

## In Texas

In Texas the lid blew off the sky a long time ago
So there's nothing to keep the wind from blowing
And it blows all the time. Everywhere is far to go
So there's no hurry at all, and no reason for going.
In Texas there's so much space words have a way
Of getting lost in the silence before they've spoken
So people hang on a long time to what they have to say;
And when they say it the silence is not broken,
But it absorbs the words and slowly gives them
Over to miles of white-gold plains and gray-green hills,
And they are part of that silence that outlives them.
Nothing moves fast in Texas except the windmills
And the hawk that rises up with a clatter of wings.
(Nothing more startling here than sudden motion,
Everything is so still.) But the earth slowly swings
In time like a great swelling never-ending ocean,
And the houses that ride the tawny waves get smaller
As you get near them because you see them then
Under the whole sky, and the whole sky is so much taller
With the lid off than a million towers built by men.
After awhile you can only see what's at horizon's edge,
And you are stretched with looking so far instead of near,
So you jump, you are startled by a blown piece of sedge;
You feel wide-eyed and ruminative as a ponderous steer.
In Texas you look at America with a patient eye.
You want everything to be sure and slow and set in relation
To immense skies and earth that never ends. You wonder why
People must talk and strain so much about a nation
That lives in spaces vaster than a man's dream and can go
Five hundred miles through wilderness, meeting only the hawk
And the dead rabbit in the road. What happens must be slow,
Must go deeper even than hand's work or tongue's talk,
Must rise out of the flesh like sweat after a hard day,
Must come slowly, in its own time, in its own way.

## Boulder Dam

Not in the cities, not among fabricated towers,
Not on the superhighways has the land been matched.
Beside the mountains, man's invention cowers.
And in a country various and wild and beautiful
How cheap the new car and the lighted movie look.
We have been hourly aware of a failure to live,
Monotonous poverty of spirit and the lack of love.

But here among hills bare and desert-red,
A violent precipice, a dizzy white curve falls
Hundreds of feet through rock to the deep canyon-bed;
A beauty sheer and clean and without error,
It stands with the created sapphire lake behind it,
It stands, a work of man as noble as the hills,
And it is faith as well as water that it spills.

Not built on terror like the empty pyramid,
Not built to conquer but to illuminate a world:
It is the human answer to a human need,
Power in absolute control, freed as a gift,
A pure creative act, God when the world was born!
It proves that we have built for life and built for love
And when we all are dead, this dam will stand and give.

## Colorado Mountains

Plain grandeur escapes definition. You
Cannot speak about the mountains well.
About the clear plane, the sharp shadow
You cannot tell.

Mountains define you. You cannot define
Them. And all your looking serves to set
What you have learned of the stern line
Against an absolute.

The frail taut structure of a human face
Beside the sheer cliff drawn, all that you loved,
All that can stand in such a bare clear place
Is to be proved.

And love that is a landscape in the past
Becomes, like mountains, changeless. It is there.
It is standing against its own image at last
In a high air.

## Of the Seasons

*Sangre de Cristo Mountains*
*Sante Fe, New Mexico*

You spoke of spring and summer
As we drove through the pinyon-spotted
Through the leopard-land, the hammer
Of sun on the bronze and the violet.
You spoke of lilies brushing
The horses' necks in spring
And dry creeks water-rushing,
"In the spring," you told me.

I remember all that you said
Of the sharp cleavage, the heat,
The cold that makes the head
Burn with an inner tension,
Sound like a glass humming.
Words break in crystal air
And silence is always coming,
"It is here," you told me.

And when you spoke of summer,
I knew the heat is in waves
And earth begins to shimmer
With violent reds and umber.
On the naked rock you told
How the fierce path of wind
Burned the structure bright as gold,
And rock fire-bare not barren,
"In the summer," you told me.

We did not speak of winter
For then we turned and saw
The sun crash and then splinter
On peaks till they were flooded
With light that aches with rose,
And all the mountains iced
Are burned again—"and those,"
You said, "are called The Blood of Christ."

## Meditation in Sunlight

In space in time I sit
Thousands of feet above
The sea and meditate
On solitude on love

Near all is brown and poor
Houses are made of earth
Sun opens every door
The city is a hearth

Far all is blue and strange
The sky looks down on snow
And meets the mountain range
Where time is light not shadow

Time in the heart held still
Space as the household god
And joy instead of will
Knows love as solitude

Knows solitude as love
Knows time as light not shadow
Thousands of feet above
The sea where I am now.

## Difficult Scene

This landscape does not speak.
Look, it is simply there,
Take it or leave it. The weak
Suffer from fierce air.

These lands—high, desolate,
Where earth is skeleton—
Make no demands; they state.
Who can resist the stone?

Implacable tranquillity
That searches out the naked heart,
Touches the quick of anxiety
And breaks the world apart.

The angel in the flaming air
Is everywhere and no escape,
Asking of life that it be pure
And given as the austere landscape.

And most accompanied when alone;
Most sensitive when mastered sense;
Alive most when the will is gone,
Absence become the greatest Presence.

# The Window

Finite, exact, the square
Frames the long curve
Of hills and perpendicular
Spray of the delicate tree.
Wires, slanting, swerve
Off the flat scene;
And shining through
The mathematical window
The burning sky and the blue sun
Create a flowing fourth dimension:
The square explodes in space.

Then through the abstract window
Darkness comes down so deep
The exact mountains show
Sleep in a flowing line,
Earth in a flowing sleep.
But suddenly alive
The rivers of the air
Invade the static square;
As the stars only move
Obedient to Love,
Heart opens into time.

The square explodes in space,
The window opens into time—
As poems breathe within their strict design,
As holiness may look out from a face.

## The Lion and the Rose

Vision is locked in stone.
The lion in the air is gone
With the great lion of the sun.
The sky is wild and cold.
The tawny fire is gone.
The hill where love did open like a rose
Is black. It snows.

Emptiness flows.
The flowers in the heart all close
Drowned in a heavy white. Love knows
That poverty untold,
The cave where nothing grows.
The flaming lions of the flesh are gone,
Their power withdrawn.

God of the empty room,
Thy will be done. Thy will be done:
Now shine the inward sun,
The beating heart that glows
Within the skeleton,
The magic rose, the purer living gold,
Shine now, grown old.

All that is young and bold,
The lion's roar, the flaming skin and wild,
Unearthly peace now cherish and enfold
And fresh sleep overcome,
That in this death-in-life, delicate, cold,
The spiritual rose
Flower among the snows—

The love surpassing love.

## Indian Dances

O have you heard it, far off, the deep drum
Calling from the Plaza all feet to come,
Calling from the Plaza the blood in the wrist
To beat with the drum, the heart in the chest
To beat with the drum, till the flesh is a fruit
That swells with the drum, and from the bone's root
Aches with the drum, till all bodies are bound
Fast to the drum and the drum to the ground,
    And the drum to the earth
    As the tree to the earth.

O have you lived in the drumbeat, the deep beat
As the old men move together, their eyelids shut fast,
Move to answer the sound of the drum in their feet
Till the song rises sweet in their old throats at last,
And springs from their throats like a river in flood
That comes from the mountains to answer the blood,
Till the flesh is a fountain and all bodies rise
Like rivers to song and the song goes to the skies,
    And the song to the sun
    As the tree to the sun.

O have you seen them, the beautiful slow dancers
Whose feet can implore the clouds for their answers,
Whose feet can converse with the ghost of the buffalo,
The light antlered deer, and remember the rainbow,
Whose feet can command the young corn to grow strong,
Whose feet spring as light from the source of the song
As the song from the rivers held secret within
And from drum bound to earth, the fruit of the skin,
    And the dance to the skies
    As the tree to the skies.

O have you heard the drumbeat and the river of song?
O have you come from far to see the grave dances?
And not known that you came to be freed by the song?
And not known that you came to be healed by the dances,
And not known that you came to witness your birth,
That you came to give back your flesh to the earth,
That you came to give back the deep rivers that rise

In the heart till it floods and pours from your eyes,
To give back the song to the clouds and the great rain,
Until you, imprisoned, are freed of your mortal pain,
    As the dead are alone and free,
    As the living when born again,
    As the tree to the earth.

## Santos: New Mexico

Return to the most human, nothing less
Will nourish the torn spirit, the bewildered heart,
The angry mind: and from the ultimate duress,
Pierced with the breath of anguish, speak for love.

Return, return to the deep sources, nothing less
Will teach the stiff hands a new way to serve,
To carve into our lives the forms of tenderness
And still that ancient necessary pain preserve.

O we have moved too far from these, all we who look
Upon the wooden painted figure, stiff and quaint,
Reading it curiously like a legend in a book—
But it is Man upon the cross. It is the living saint.

To those who breathed their faith into the wood
It was no image, but the very living source,
The savior of their own humanity by blood
That flows terribly like a river in its course.

They did not fear the strangeness, nor while gazing
Keep from this death their very precious life.
They looked until their hands and hearts were blazing
And the reality of pain pierced like a knife.

We must go down into the dungeons of the heart,
To the dark places where modern mind imprisons
All that is not defined and thought apart.
We must let out the terrible creative visions.

Return to the most human, nothing less
Will teach the angry spirit, the bewildered heart,
The torn mind, to accept the whole of its duress,
And pierced with anguish, at last act for love.

## Poet in Residence

*Carbondale, Illinois*

### The Students

I looked behind you for the towers of music,
And for the remembered words, blue hills of childhood;
What human mind had touched yours to the quick?
What passions, hungers streamed through your blood?
Had you been Marie Curie or Keats or some sad queen
Dying in great pomp and pride alone?

> Your grandfathers were huge with dreams,
> Crossed an ocean and half a continent, breathing hope;
> When corn failed further North after a drought,
> Migrated down to this hot and fertile land
> And named it Little Egypt, Bible in hand;
> Brought with them a tradition of fierce work,
> Saw cities rise in the wilderness, Thebes and Cairo,
> Governed themselves, invented States and rules,
> Imagined the marvelous rich life sure to grow
> When the ground was cleared, the hard work done,
> And on summer evenings, sitting Bible in hand,
> Dreamed of a great teacher or poet grandson.

I looked behind you for the towers of music
And found only the broken jazz record
And last week's magazine gone stale,
An old moan and a blurred word,
A flat face with no deepening scene behind it:
You remember the portraits of the Renaissance,
The face and then behind it the mysterious scene—
The secret river, the soft green unemphatic hill
Where everyone has been and no one has been.
Literature is like this, you know, philosophy
And music have this effect on the personality,
Set behind it a magical, a marvelous world,
Open it up, enlarge it, fill with wild excitement—
But ignorant of man's long ecstasy and pain,

You come to books as to a strange dull town
Where you know no one by name and do not care,
And never recognize the Waste Land as your own.

I looked behind you and saw nothing, nothing at all,
But a flat empty wall,
I saw you lonely and bored walking in a dull town;
I saw you letting the books fall.
And then because there was nothing else to do,
I saw you turning on the radio.

## Campus

Yes, I have been lonely, angry here,
Lonely on the suffocating walks under the trees
Where faces cross and recross bright with sweat,
And damp hands clutch the books unmarked by love.
Intricate and empty this crisscross movement
Through the green, through the bird song
As if it were a dance but with no meaning,
And I, the stranger, often lit up by anger,
Waiting for someone to ask the simple question,
"Why have you come and who are you, stranger?"
And to say gladly, "Nothing but a voice,
Nothing but an angry joy, a protestation,
Nothing, a gift of nothing on the desolate air—"
Here in the center of America
Steeped deep in the tiger-lily June
Where the iced blue Hydrangea
Cuts the air like a tune
Here where the parched bird is still at noon,
Here in the center of Amereica where it is always noon,
On the secure sidewalks of the typical town,
I go alone and a stranger, a haunted walker,
Full of self-questioning and wonder,
Waiting for the speech, for the word
To break the tension like a clap of thunder,
"How can the books be broken to yield the dynamic answer,
And we embody thought in living as does the dance, the dancer?"

### Before Teaching

These nights when the frog grates shrilly by the pond
And fireflies' points of flame flicker the gloom,
Where birds are stilled in the dense thicket-heat,
And I have seen through haze a bloody moon
Rise through the trees to make the sober town
A legendary place, a place of fearful glory,
These nights when, knowing I shall have to teach
When morning comes again, are close to fear,
I ask myself, fumbling and full of doubt, angry with time,
How stamp for you as if a gold coin in relief
The single signature of passion and belief?

What through the years endures, the only joy,
The one delight age does increase, the discipline
That fosters growth within it and is ever fertile,
And the great freedom too that comes with this—
And if I cannot do it, why be a poet then,
Or talk of art, or weep for its defeat?
These nights the frog grates and the firefly
Pricks the dense thickets of the gloomy heat
Have known the heart's will and its savage cry,
And too the delicate cool wind, the blessing on the air.

### After Teaching

I am only beginning to know what I was taught
As a child about poetry, about life, about myself;
It takes a long time for words to become thought,
For thought, the slow burner, to burn through
Into life where it can scorch the palm of a hand,
When what was merely beautiful or strange
Suffers the metamorphosis, the blood-change,
Looks out of eyes or walks down the street,
All that was abstract become concrete,
Is part of you like an eyelash or your hair;
You say "Poetry" and mean you have been there.
You are just beginning to understand
What it is all about, the imaginary land,

Say, "I can't possibly describe the weather.
It's as if the sky burned, was all on fire,
Ecstasy that makes ash of bodily desire—
But all I have to show is a stone and a blue feather."

My children, you with whom I have learned so much,
Do not turn back to these hours; go forward,
Look to the fertile days and years ahead
When all that meaning and its implication,
The full tone and the half-tone and the whisper
Will sound together and keep the mind awake,
As after hearing a difficult quartet
The theme comes clear and you listen again
Long after you had thought you heard;
So it is with the deep thought, the deep word.
Now we are able only to graph the flight,
For we never actually rose from the ground.
Imagine a moment when student and teacher
(Long after the day and the lesson are over)
Will soar together to the pure immortal air
And finds Yeats, Hopkins, Eliot waiting there.

But you understand, it cannot happen yet.
It takes a long time to live what you learn:
I believe we shall meet again and show each other
These curious marvels, the stone and the blue feather;
And we shall meet again when your own children are
Taught what they will not know for many a year.

## Place of Learning

Heavy, heavy the summer and its gloom,
The place, a place of learning, the difficult strange place,
And for what reason and from how far did you come,
To find the desolation and the thin soil,
To find the great heat and the sudden rain,
To listen for the long cry of the through train?

The time, a time of teaching, a curious time.

The birds alone made welcome in the morning sun
And all else strange. But this familiar, this well known,

This, in a sense, always the world where one moves
Opening the doors, opening the doors to push through alone,
And it is a way of many isolated deepening loves.
This we have known. It has been like this before.
The place of learning. The fear and trembling. The final opening
    of a door.

But here in the place of learning, in the time of teaching,
To find also, and surely not by accident,
Among the gifts of trees, of birds, the various gifts:
Coolness after long heat, a lightening sky after
Much heaviness, also to find—
The open heart, detached and open,
So feeling it has become impersonal as sunlight,
To find this curious one, creative and aloof:
From how far and for what reason did you come,
Stranger with a fire in your head, to this deep kind of welcome?

So what you gave was given and what you taught was learned,
Striking rock for water and the water falling from air,
Opening a door to find someone in the room, already there.

# The Work of Happiness

I thought of happiness, how it is woven
Out of the silence in the empty house each day
And how it is not sudden and it is not given
But is creation itself like the growth of a tree.
No one has seen it happen, but inside the bark
Another circle is growing in the expanding ring.
No one has heard the root go deeper in the dark,
But the tree is lifted by this inward work
And its plumes shine, and its leaves are glittering.

So happiness is woven out of the peace of hours
And strikes its roots deep in the house alone:
The old chest in the corner, cool waxed floors,
White curtains softly and continually blown
As the free air moves quietly about the room;
A shelf of books, a table, and the white-washed wall—
These are the dear familiar gods of home,
And here the work of faith can best be done,
The growing tree is green and musical.

For what is happiness but growth in peace,
The timeless sense of time when furniture
Has stood a life's span in a single place,
And as the air moves, so the old dreams stir
The shining leaves of present happiness?
No one has heard thought or listened to a mind,
But where people have lived in inwardness
The air is charged with blessing and does bless;
Windows look out on mountains and the walls are kind.

## After a Train Journey

My eyes are full of rivers and trees tonight,
The clear waters sprung in the green,
The swan's neck flashing in sunlight,
The trees laced dark, the tiny unknown flowers,
Skies never still, shining and darkening the hours.
How can I tell you all that I have been?

My thoughts are rooted with the trees,
My thoughts flow with the stream.
They flow and are arrested as a frieze.
How can I answer now or tell my dream,
How tell you what is far and what is near?
Only that river, tree and swan are here.

Even at the slow rising of the full moon,
That delicate disturber of the soul,
I am so drenched in rivers and in trees,
I cannot speak. I have nothing to tell,
Except that I must learn of this pure solitude
All that I am and might be, root and bone,
Flowing and still and beautiful and good,
Now I am almost earth and almost whole.

## O Who Can Tell?

What is experience, O who can tell?
Is it the senses holding the real world
To the heart's ear as hands hold up a shell
To listen to the wave furled and unfurled?

What is it? Mind's invention, human treasure,
An alchemy that plucks out juy from suffering,
Finds the hard stone at the core of pleasure,
Gently withdraws from guilt its waspish sting?

Is it the image, eyelid-flicker snapped
When lovers in suspension in the air
Know in one glance an island-world is mapped
Which each will secretly develop later?

The word is "later" when the senses yield
The meditative heart their curious plunder.
The inference is silence, where, distilled,
The wave unfurls and falls, translated wonder.

## The Clavichord

She keeps her clavichord
As others keep delight, too light
To breathe, the secret word
No lover ever heard
Where the pure spirit lives
And garlands weaves.

To make the pure notes sigh
(Not of a human grief, too brief)
A sigh of such fragility
Her fingers' sweet agility
Must hold the horizontal line
In the stern power of design.

The secret breathed within
And never spoken, woken
By music; the garlands in
Her hands no one has seen.
She wreathes the air with green
And weaves the stillness in.

## Song

Now let us honor with violin and flute
A woman set so deeply in devotion
That three times blasted to the root
Still she grew green and poured strength out.

Still she stood fair, providing the cool shade,
Compassion, the thousand leaves of mercy,
The cherishing green hope. Still like a tree she stood,
Clear comfort in the town and all the neighborhood.

Pure as the tree is pure, young
As the tree forever young, magnanimous
And natural, sweetly serving: for her the song,
For her the flute sound and the violin be strung.
        For her all love, all praise,
        All honor, as for trees
        In the hot summer days.

# In Memoriam

*Veglio, penso, ardo, piange*
Petrarch

## I

Think, weep, love, O watch
This casket that no keys unlatch
And may your eyes once locked in her
Gently release their prisoner.

Watch, love, weep, O think
Till it is thought not tears you drink
And thought can keep all pain apart
From her dissolved and open heart.

Love, watch, think, O weep
For her no love nor watch could keep
And may your tears be the release
Of what kept you not her from peace.

Weep, think, watch, O love
Her who lies here and cannot move
And may your love rest lightly on
Her quiet consummation.

## II

Only the purest voices,
The formal, the most disciplined,
Those that spring fully armed
From the dark caverns of the mind
Can stand beside her name,
Bright crystal, not bright flame.

And when those inward rivers rise
And flood your outward-looking eyes,
Wring the essential oils from pain:
Go back to Mozart once again,
Play Beethoven's great Emperor,
Play Monteverdi, Bach for her.
Hear trumpet Milton and the flutes of Marvell:
Triumph not grief is what they have to tell.

The mastery that comes from discipline,
The joy that springs from form
(Where fumbling and facility are sin)
This was her element, her power, her charm—
On luminous and stern foundations
Built her detached, creative meditations.

Now fling the arches high and far from grief,
The light-swung bridges of your work and days.
Live now with knowledge, with compassion, and with praise.
Wherever spirit triumphs is her faith designed,
"By this great light upon our mind."

## Now Voyager

Now voyager, lay here your dazzled head.
Come back to earth from air, be nourishèd,
Not with that light on light, but with this bread.

Here close to earth be cherished, mortal heart,
Hold your way deep as roots push rocks apart
To bring the spurt of green up from the dark.

Where music thundered let the mind be still,
Where the will triumphed let there be no will,
What light revealed now let the dark fulfill.

Here close to earth the deeper pulse is stirred,
Here where no wings rush and no sudden bird,
But only heartbeat upon beat is heard.

Here let the fiery burden be all spilled,
The passionate voice at last be calmed and stilled
And the long yearning of the blood fulfilled.

Now voyager, come home, come home to rest,
Here on the long-lost country of earth's breast
Lay down the fiery vision and be blest, be blest.

## My Sisters, O My Sisters

*Nous qui voulions poser, image ineffaceable*
*Comme un delta divin notre main sur le sable*
                                        Anna de Noailles

### I

Dorothy Wordsworth, dying, did not want to read,
"I am too busy with my own feelings," she said.

And all women who have wanted to break out
Of the prison of consciousness to sing or shout

Are strange monsters who renounce the treasure
Of their silence for a curious devouring pleasure.

Dickinson, Rossetti, Sappho—they all know it,
Something is lost, strained, unforgiven in the poet.

She abdicates from life or like George Sand
Suffers from the mortality in an immortal hand,

Loves too much, spends a whole life to discover
She was born a good grandmother, not a good lover.

Too powerful for men: Madame de Stael. Too sensitive:
Madame de Sévigné, who burdened where she meant to give.

Delicate as that burden was and so supremely lovely,
It was too heavy for her daughter, much too heavy.

Only when she built inward in a fearful isolation
Did any one succeed or learn to fuse emotion

With thought. Only when she renounced did Emily
Begin in the fierce lonely light to learn to be.

Only in the extremity of spirit and the flesh
And in renouncing passion did Sappho come to bless.

Only in the farewells or in old age does sanity
Shine through the crimson stains of their mortality.

And now we who are writing women and strange monsters
Still search our hearts to find the difficult answers,

Still hope that we may learn to lay our hands
More gently and more subtly on the burning sands.

To be through what we make more simply human,
To come to the deep place where poet becomes woman,

Where nothing has to be renounced or given over
In the pure light that shines out from the lover,

In the pure light that brings forth fruit and flower
And that great sanity, that sun, the feminine power.

## II

Let us rejoice in
The full curve of breast,
The supple thigh
And all riches in
A woman's keeping
For man's comfort and rest
(Crimson and ivory)
For children's nourishment
(Magic fruits and flowers).
But when they are sleeping,
The children, the men,
Fed by these powers,
We know what is meant
By the wise serpent,
By the gentle dove,
And remember then
How we wish to love,

Let us rejoice now
In these great powers
Which are ours alone.
And trust what we know:
First the green hand
That can open flowers
In the deathly bone,
And the magic breast
That can feed the child,
And is under a hand

A rose of fire in snow
So tender, so wild
All fires come to rest,
All lives can be blest—
So sighs the gentle dove,
Wily the serpent so,
Matched in a woman's love.

## III

Eve and Mary the mother are our stem;
All our centuries go back to them.
And delicate the balance lies
Between the passionate and wise:
Of man's rib, one, and cleaves to him;
And one bears man and then frees him.
This double river has created us,
Always the rediscovered, always the cherished.
(But many fail in this. Many have perished.)

Hell is the loss of balance when woman is destroyer.
Each of us has been there.
Each of us knows what the floods can do.
How many women mother their husbands
Out of all strength and secret *Virtu*;
How many women love an only son
As a lover loves, binding the free hands.
How many yield up their true power
Out of weakness, the moment of passion
Betrayed by years of confused living—
For it is surely a lifetime work,
This learning to be a woman.
Until at the end what is clear
Is the marvelous skill to make
Life grow in all its forms.

Is knowing where to ask, where to yield,
Where to sow, where to plough the field,
Where to kill the heart or let it live;
To be Eve, the giver of knowledge, the lover;
To be Mary, the shield, the healer and the mother.

The balance is eternal whatever we may wish;
The law can be broken but we cannot change
What is supremely beautiful and strange.
Where find the root? Where re-join the source?
The fertile feminine goddess, double river?

## IV

We think of all the women hunting for themselves,
Turning and turning to each other with a driving
Need to learn to understand, to live in charity,
And above all to be used fully, to be giving
From wholeness, wholeness back to love's deep clarity.
O, all the burning hearts of women unappeased
Shine like great stars, like flowers of fire,
As the sun goes and darkness opens all desire—
And we are with a fierce compassion seized.
How lost, how far from home, how parted from
The earth, my sisters, O my sisters, we have come!

For so long asked so little of ourselves and men,
And let the Furies have their way—our treasure,
The single antidote to all our world's confusion,
A few gifts to the poor small god of pleasure.
The god of passion has gone back into the mountain,
Is sleeping in the dark, deep in the earth.

We have betrayed a million times the holy fountain,
The potent spirit who brings his life to birth,
The masculine and violent joy of pure creation—
And yielded up the sacred fires to sensation.
But we shall never come home to the earth
Until we bring the great god and his mirth
Back from the mountain, until we let this stranger
Plough deep into our hearts his joy and anger,
For we shall never find ourselves again
Until we ask mens' greatness back from men,
And we shall never find ourselves again
Until we match mens' greatness with our own.

# The Lady and the Unicorn

## *The Cluny Tapestries*

I am the unicorn and bow my head
You are the lady woven into history
And here forever we are bound in mystery
Our wine, Imagination, and our bread,
And I the unicorn who bows his head.

You are all interwoven in my history
And you and I have been most strangely wed
I am the unicorn and bow my head
And lay my wildness down upon your knee
You are the lady woven into history.

And here forever we are sweetly wed
With flowers and rabbits in the tapestry
You are the lady woven into history
Imagination is our bridal bed:
We lie ghostly upon it, no word said.

Among the flowers of the tapestry
I am the unicorn and by your bed
Come gently, gently to bow down my head,
Lay at your side this love, this mystery,
And call you lady of my tapestry.

I am the unicorn and bow my head
To one so sweetly lost, so strangely wed:

You sit forever under a small formal treee
Where I forever search your eyes to be

Rewarded with this shining tragedy
And know your beauty was not cast for me,

Know we are woven all in mystery,
The wound imagined where no one has bled,

My wild love chastened to this history
Where I before your eyes, bow down my head.

## Question

I saw the world in your face
And it was fearful loneliness,
As if the self were in disgrace;
I saw the heart of emptiness
And thought that I was fashioned then
To be the mirror of your pain.

To be the witness only, be
The mirror, the crystalline eye
That treats grief as anatomy
To read the world's ill by,
The haunted witness of
Our lack of love, our lack of love.

But now I move with you as one,
The ghost within your skeleton,
And ask and ask the only question:
How can we live and this go on?
How shall the naked starving soul
Be fed, be clothed, and be made whole?

My child, my world, my dear,
Balm of my heart, joy so severe
You hold within a single tear
All of our human anguish clear,
How will this arduous joy you have
Be yours, be mine, witthout your love?

When will you give yourself all that you are,
O world of pain, O lucid morning star?

## Perspective

Now I am coming toward you silently,
Do not say anything. Stay as you are—
Suspense between my love and your despair.
Like a stone figure on a fountain, be
The center of an arc of paths and trees.
Now I am coming toward you, freeze!
Be nothing but yourself, not even mine,
You as you are when all alone and free,
Suspended outside love and outside time—
Look at me as I am, as if I were a tree.
Now I am coming toward you, say nothing,
Shine in your own light, purer than my joy,
And I shall, coming toward you, make no cry,
But try to sense the nearness and the space
Between my windswept leaves and your still face,
Between the tree and the stone figure drawn
Together, if at all, by shadow or some simple dawn.

# Return

It is time I came back to my real life
After this voyage to an island with no name,
Where I lay down at sunrise drunk with light.

Here are books, paper, and my little knife,
The walls of solitude from which I came,
Here is the sobering, meditative night,

The quiet room where it is dark and cool
After the intense green and the flame,
The flat white walls, the table are each good.

Long hours of work and the imposed rule:
That was the time of the tremendous rain,
The place of lightning, of the great flood.

This is the time when voyagers return
With a mad longing for known customs and things,
Where joy in an old pencil is not absurd.

What was fire is music. Then the heart was torn.
But tears are indulgence. Memory sings.
I speak of an island. Passion is the word.

## "O Saisons! O Châteaux!"

When I landed it was coming home,
Home to all anguish, conflict and all love,
The heart stretched as the seasons move,
Summer is white roses and purple foxglove,
Spring was a crimson tulip standing alone.
    We only keep what we lose.

O seasons, O castles, O splendor of trees!
The star of avenues and the triumphant square,
And in the Metro once a woman with red hair,
The weary oval face and tense France there,
Too few roots now, too many memories.
    We only keep what we lose.

The dark gloom of the forest and my dream,
The clouds that make the sky a tragic spell
And windows that frame partings in a well:
You bent down from a balcony to say farewell.
Across lost landscapes the trains scream.
    We only keep what we lose.

Parting freezes the image, roots the heart.
Once spring was a tulip standing alone,
Summer is a forest of roses and green.
No one will see again what I have seen.
And I possess you now from whom I part:
    We only keep what we lose.

## These Pure Arches

*A Painting by Chirico*
*"The Delights of the Poet"*

Here space, time, peace are given a habitation,
Perspective of pillar and arch, shadow on light,
A luminous evening where it can never be night.
This is the pure splendor of imagination.

To hold eternally present and forever still
The always fugitive, to make the essence clear,
Compose time and the moment as shadow in a square,
As these pure arches have been composed by will.

As by a kind of absence, feat of supersession
We can evoke a face long lost, long lost in death,
Or those hidden now in the wilderness of oppression—
Know the immortal breath upon the mortal breath:

A leaping out of the body to think, the sense
Of absence that precedes the stern work of creation.
Now when the future depends on our imagination,
Remember these pure arches and their imminence.

# We Have Seen the Wind

*New England Hurricane, 1938*

We have seen the wind and we need not be warned.
It is no plunderer of roses. It is nothing sweet.
We have seen the torturer of trees, O we have learned
How it bends them, how it wrenches at their rooted feet,
Till the earth cracks like a cake round their torn feet.

We saw the strong trees struggle and their plumes go down,
The poplar bend and whip back till it split to fall,
The elm tear up at the root and topple like a crown,
The pine crack at the base—we had to watch them all.
The ash, the lovely cedar. We had to watch them fall.

They went so softly under the loud flails of air,
Before that fury they went down like feathers,
With all the hundred springs that flowered in their hair,
And all the years, endured in all the weathers—
To fall as if they were nothing, as if they were feathers.

Do not speak to us of the wind. We know now. We know.
We do not need any more of destruction than all these,
These that were proud and great and still so swift to go,
Do not speak to us any more of the carnage of the trees,
Lest the heart remember other dead than these—

Lest the heart split like a tree from root to crown,
And bearing all its springs, like a feather go down.

## Homage to Flanders

Country of still canals, green willows, golden fields, all
Laid like a carpet for majestic winds to tread,
Where peace is in the lines of trees, but overhead
Heaven is marching: low lands where winds are tall,

Small lands where skies are the huge houses of the lark,
Rich lands where men are poor and reap what they have sown,
Who plant the small hugged acre where each works alone,
Men who rise with the sun and sleep with the early dark.

These are the country's marrow, these who work the land,
Passionate partisans and arguers, but who still go on,
Whoever governs, planting the same seed under the same sun,
These who hold Flanders like a plough in the hand.

Their feet are rooted in earth but their hearts are moody,
Close to the dark skies, wind never still in their ears—
They were the battlefield of Europe for five hundred years.
The thunder may be guns. The skirts of the wind are bloody.

This land, this low land under threatening skies,
This Flanders full of skulls, has set a fury in the slow
Hearts of its people that, taking centuries to grow,
Now burns with a certain violence in their eyes.

It has made their land a passion which they must save
In every generation, spilling their blood to hold it.
Dogged and avaricious, they have never sold it.
Proud and fierce it has kept them. It has kept them brave,

Given their language coarseness, and a great breath
Of soldiers' laughter from the belly and a flood
Of poetry that flows like war in the stream of their blood,
Slow and melancholy and half in love with death.

This was my father's country and the country of my birth,
And isn't it a strange thing that, after the deliberate mind
Has yielded itself wholly to another land, stubborn and blind,
The heart gives its secret homage still to Flemish earth?

I knew it when I was seven after the war and years of slumber:
The Flemish self awoke as we entered the Scheldt, and suddenly
The tears rushed to my eyes, though all we could see
Was a low land under a huge sky that I did not remember.

# The Sacred Order

*For George Sarton*

Never forget this when the talk is clever:
Michelet suffered chaos in his bone
To bring to clarity the history of France.
His life-blood flowed into old documents.
The scholar at his desk burned like a lover.

At century's end behold the sceptic rules;
Doubt, like the tyrant's servants, seals
The visionary books. The scholar's passion,
His burning heart is wholly out of fashion.
The human spirit goes, the caste prevails.

Now is detachment the supreme holy word
(Above all take no part nor risk your head);
Forgotten are Erasmus' pilgrimages
By these who fabricate and love their cages—
Has truth then never buckled on a sword?

Never forget this when the talk is clever:
Wisdom must be born in the flesh or wither,
And sacred order has been always won
From chaos by some burning faithful one
Whose human bones have ached as if with fever

To bring you to these high triumphant places.
Forget the formulas, remember men.
Praise scholars, for their never-ending story
Is written out in fire and this is their glory.
Read faith as on a lover's in their faces.

## What the Old Man Said

*For Lugné-Poe, founder of the Oeuvre Theatre in Paris*

At sixty-five said, "I fight every day.
My dear, nothing but death will stop
My uninterrupted élan in the play."
Then wrote, "When I am forced to see
What happens to our old humanity,
All seems ignoble and I rage
To have been listed player on this stage."
At sixty-five that anger conquered fear:
The old man raged, but he did not despair.

At sixty-seven then he laughed and said,
"My dear, how proud I am of all the haters
Who stand behind and wish that I were dead,"
Those who had tasted of his honesty,
Those usurers of mediocrity—
At sixty-seven he refused to praise
(And lost his job) their rotten little plays.
But when he told me how he shouted there,
The old man laughed, but he did not despair.

At seventy said, "We must work, my dear.
I see a certain look upon their faces.
Discouragement? Perhaps I dream it there.
The wicked times have put me back to school,
And I shall die a sensitive young fool.
The news is doing me to death at last."
And then a note, "The evil eats me fast.
You must help men not to be slaves, my dear!"
(The old man died, but he did not despair.)

## Navigator

This lazy prince of tennis balls and lutes,
Marvelous redhead who could eat and have his cake,
Collector of hot jazz, Japanese prints, rare books,
The charming winner who takes all for the game's sake,
Is now disciplined, changed, and wrung into a man.
For war's sake, in six months, this can be done.

Now he is groomed and cared for like a fighting cock,
His blood enriched, his athlete's nerve refined
In crucibles of tension to be electric under shock,
His intellect composed for action and designed
To map a bomber's passage to Berlin by stars,
Precision's instrument that neither doubts nor fears.

This can be done in six months. Take a marvelous boy
And knead him into manhood for destruction's joy.
This can be done in six months, but we never tried
Until we needed the lute player's sweet lifeblood.
O the composed mind and the electric nerve
Were never trained like this to build, to love, to serve.

Look at him now and swear by every bomb he will release,
This shall be done. This shall be better done in peace!

# Who Wakes

### *Detroit, June 1943*

Who wakes now who lay blind with sleep?
Who starts bright-eyed with anger from his bed?
I do. I, the plain citizen. I cannot sleep.
I hold the torturing fire in my head.

I, an American, call the dead Negro's name,
And in the hot dark of the city night
I walk the streets alone and sweat with shame.
Too late to rise, to raise the dead too late.

This is the harvest. The seeds sown long ago—
The careless word, sly thought, excusing glance.
I reap now everything I let pass, let go.
This is the harvest of my own indifference.

I, the plain citizen, have grown disorder
In my own world. It is not what I meant.
But dreams and images are potent and can murder.
I stand accused of them. I am not innocent.

Can I now plant imagination, honesty,
And love, where violence and terror were unbound—
The images of hope, the dream's responsibility?

Those who died here were murdered in my mind.

## Return to Chartres

We came to Chartres, riding the green plain,
The spear of hope, the incorruptible towers,
The great tree rooted in the heart of France
Blazing eternally with sacred flowers;
We came to Chartres, the house without a stain,
The mastery of passion by belief,
With all its aspiration held in balance;
We came to Chartres, the magic spear of grain,
The spear of wheat forever nourishing,
The never-wasted stalk, the ever blessing.

And there we meditated on our tragic age,
Split at the heart, flowering without a stem,
For we are barren men haunted by rage
Who cannot find our hope here though we came,
Now all the hope we have is human love:
Passion without belief destroys our love.

## To the Living

### I

Now we must kill or perish, desolate choice—
Indifference not hatred brought us to this place.
There was a time when charity still had a voice.

There was a time for love's imaginative face
And healing touch, for the deep searching eyes
That may behold the miracles of grace.

We could have beaten down the dangerous lies
If we had helped the helpless in their lonely stand,
And made a real peace, peace where no one dies,

And never watched the hearts spilt out on sand,
The best and dearest, the innumerable lost,
Nor come too late, too late to understand.

Now we must pay the full, the fearful cost,
Now we must fight the war we could have won
Without becoming what we hated most.

Now we must kill or perish. It is done.
And we fight for ourselves with little grace;
Who sold out human lives, now spend our own.

But through destruction fight back to the place
Where in the end the pure and healing touch,
The searching eyes and love's long hidden face,

Turning toward us in our self-made desolation,
May teach us all through suffering so much
What might have been learned through imagination.

### II

Who is the refugee,
The homesick one,
Climbing the long stairs of exile
And always alone?

Who is the wanderer,
At peace nowhere,

The burning leaf before hot winds
Blown here and there?

Who is the sick stranger
Whose thirst no well
In all the world can slake,
Nor fever, cool?

Who is the poor beggar
Bound in a cart
To wander everlasting desert sand
And eat his heart?

That thirst, that hunger and that homesickness,
The lonely burning day and sleepness night,
When all seemed desert-waste and bitterness
To be escaped in flight—

That never was escape, nor rest, nor sleep
But only long pursuit and pain—
Who has not known it? Who so wholly blest
Such loneliness could be to him unknown?

Each is an exile from the whole. The agony
Of separation is the human agony.
From the four corners of the earth
How bring us home into humanity?

How bring us home, how bring us home at last,
Who bear the old divisions of the past,
The ancient hatreds and the ancient evils
Held in the heart as if a thousand devils?
How exorcize, how purify, how bless
This fearful universal loneliness?

### III

How faint the horn sounds in the mountain passes
Where, folded in the folds of memory,
All the heroic helmets lie in summer grasses,
Who wore them vanished utterly.

How dry the blood on ancient cross and stone
Where, folded in the folds of memory,

The martyrs cry out where each falls alone
In his last faithful agony.

How fresh and clear the stains of human weeping
Where, folded in the folds of memory,
The millions who have died for us are sleeping
In our long tragic history.

## IV

The need to kill what is unknown and strange
Whether it be a poem or an ancient race,
The fear of thought, fear of experience
That might demand some radical heart-change—
These are the mountains that hem a narrow place
Out of the generous plains of our inheritance:
Speak to the children of the world as whole,
Whole as the heart that can include it all,
And of the fear of thought as the first sin;
Tell them the revolution is within.

Open the mind, and the whole earth and sky
Are freed from fear to be explored and known.
Nothing so strange it does not hold delight
Once it is seen with clear and naked eye.
The thinking man will never be alone—
He travels where he sits, his heart alight:
Speak to the children of a living Greece
As real as Texas, and the whole earth a place
Where everywhere men hope and work to be
More greatly human and responsible and free.

Tell them the deepest changes rise like rivers
From hearts of men long dead; tell them that we
Are borne now on the currents of their faith—
The saints and martyrs and all great believers,
As well at Rome with Paul as at Thermopylae:
Our freedom rises from the body of this death.
Tell them the rivers are rich to overflowing
And as we love our fraction of the past in growing
These floods of change are to be loved and cherished;
That we may live, millions of men have perished.

Give them their rich, their full inheritance:
Open the whole past and see the future plain—
The long treks across China, all the voyages.
Look deep and know these were not done by chance.
Look far enough ahead and see the fruits of pain,
And see the harvests of all pilgrimages:
Speak to the children now of revolution
Not as a violence, a terror, and a dissolution,
But as the long-held hope and the long dream of man,
The river in his heart and his most pure tradition.

## The Tortured

Cried Innocence, "Mother, my thumbs, my thumbs!
The pain will make me wild."
And Wisdom answered, "Your brother-man
Is suffering, my child."

Screamed Innocence, "Mother, my eyes, my eyes!
Someone is blinding me."
And Wisdom answered, "Those are your brother's eyes,
The blinded one is he."

Cried Innocence, "Mother, my heart, my heart!
It bursts with agony."
And Wisdom answered, "That is your brother's heart
Breaking upon a tree."

Screamed Innocence, "Mother, I want to die.
I cannot bear the pain."
And Wisdom answered, "They will not let him die.
They bring him back again."

Cried Innocence, "Mother, I cannot bear
It now. My flesh is wild!"
And Wisdom answered, "His agony is endless
For your sake, my child."

Then whispered Innocence, "Mother, forgive
Forgive my sin, forgive—"
And Wisdom wept. "Now do you understand, Love,
How you must live?"

## The Birthday

What shall we give The Child this day,
On this shining day
In a starving world,
What gifts, what toys, for this, Love's dearest birthday?

For gold, give the heart's hunger,
The heart's want give for myrrh,
For hunger and want are stronger
And purer and deeper than anything
We have, than any joy we sing.

These and one more, the third,
These and one saving grace,
The balsam-scented word,
Green in the desolate place;
Give to His Innocence
Our hope for frankincense.

Now lay down thirst and hunger
There in the lonely manger,
And in the desolate place
Lay the green saving grace,
The bough without a thorn,
For God in man is born;
Out of all grief and pain,
Love, be renewed again!

# The Leaves of the Tree
## (1948–1950)

# Myth

The temple stood, holy and perfect,
Each pillar bearing its limit of strain serenely,
Balance and order shining in the dark.

And then a rush of swans' wings in the air,
A shower of stars. Thunder. All cracked apart.
Disorder of marble. Pockets of violet shadow.
Strange black gashes filled with the thrust of flowers.
The single arch which had enclosed the heart
Split open to the huge arches of the dark.

There was a rush of swans' wings through the air.

And those who had built the temple with such care
Came to a splendor of ruins,
Saw the perspectives altered
And all the pillars thrown to the ground,
And silent in their astonishment,
Learned what the gods can do.

## Song without Music

The lady said to her lover,
"I have given you all the bridges
Over the Seine, the old and the new,
Do you ask more, O stranger,
With your fierce hunger?"
The lover said to his lady,
"Every day your eyes are blue."

The lady said to her lover,
"I have given you all the trees
In Paris, the young and the old,
What more do you want, O boy,
With your hungry joy?"
The lover said to his lady,
"Every day your hair is gold."

The lady said to her lover,
"I have given you Notre Dame,
Three angels in three days.
What more do you want, strange child,
Importunate and wild?"
The lover said to his lady,
"Every day your mouth is praise."

The lady looked at her lover.
She gave him her mouth and her hair,
And her blue eyes were black.
"What more can I, unicorn,
That still your heart is torn?"
And her lover bowed his horn
And gave the presents back:

"The blue, the gold, the praise,
All bridges and all trees,
Three angels in three days,
And I am still forlorn.
Oh, we are heartbreak, you and I,
As written in the tapestry,
And all the presents you can give
Will never feed my hungry love."

## The Swans

I think this was a dream, and yet we saw
The stone bridge and the still canal,
And I remember how laburnum threw
A gold rain on the water very well—
After all, what we saw may have been true.

There in a rocky angle the two swans
On a small platform fashioned like a stage
In all that watery world were rooted ones,
And face to face, the snowy double image
Stood entranced there among the ancient stones.

Then as we watched the ritual play began;
They arched their wings full-span and shivered once,
Then gravely bowed their heads, and swan to swan
Lifted their heavy bodies in the dance,
Their long necks sinuous upon the silence,

Their long necks writing figures on the air
As if, like skates on ice, their beaks must draw
A precise pattern, and, what was written there,
Repeated with a concentrated awe,
Until the tension seemed too great to bear.

In one ecstatic motion, straight and pure,
The weaving necks were lifted, and each now
Stretched to the sky, as if it could endure
The little space between them better so,
And trembled! How immaculate they were!

Who would not pray, looking at such a scene,
To be alive, passionate, part of the dance,
And gladly yielding up all that is human
Become a part of natural delight for once,
Lovers take on the grave shape of the swan?

# The Second Spring

At the bottom of the green field she lies,
Abandoned foreground to the rooted trees,
To the house and children; in her open eyes
The birds' wings flash; there is a hum of bees
In the air overhead, in the flowers of the lime.
She is a plant. Without words, she speaks;
Without moving, grows; lives without time.
Has she been there for days, perhaps for weeks?

At the bottom of the green field she lies,
Without moving, moves. She becomes a stream.
Clouds pass in and out of her open eyes
And no one knows the content of this dream.
She has become a source, mysterious flow
That is forever rooted and forever passes,
The ripple of silence, infinitely slow.
She lies as if asleep down in the grasses.

When will the diviner be sent for, to strike
The hidden source with his wand, and there the wand
Leap out of his hands as the waters wake,
She wake from her dream, alive and stunned,
The heart shape transparent in her breast,
And listen to its voice, buried so deep
She does not hear, nor know how far from sleep,
How far this intense growth is from rest.

At the bottom of the green field she lies
Deep in the spring, lost in its mysteries.

## Kot's House

If the house is clean and pure,
Fiercely incorruptible,
God is ever at the door,
The Father and the Prodigal.

Should He never be aware
Of the order of each plate,
Still they will be shining there
And the floor immaculate.

Though at times the things revolt,
Fickle water or damp wall,
The chipped cup or stiffened bolt
(Love, where is your Prodigal?)

Still the house waits and is glad;
Every tea cup is a welcome,
Every cup aspires to God
Even if He never come.

And whether He exist at all,
The Father and the Prodigal,
He is expected by these things
And each plate Hosannah sings!

## To an Honest Friend

Thank God for honesty and anger
And let soft words go hang,
For there is more good danger,
More thrust in honest words
Than in love's lightly handled swords
Or the song the sirens sang.

You'll never be my stranger,
O dear destructive friend;
The truth lasts so much longer
Than beauty or than charm.
It cannot break or come to harm
And it will never end.

So thank God for your honesty
For when all's done and said,
We build on rock though bitterly,
And friendship follows after
With its ironic laughter
When truth is brought to bed.

## Landscape Pursued by a Cloud

Outside the wind tears at the trees;
Dark comes into this room like a stranger
And we are touched by a huge loneliness.
The quiet evening has its special danger,
The shape of the heart filling the empty room.
Outside is wilderness, the terrible hills.
Look out, it comes to burst open the door,
Burst in on the books, the game of solitaire,
Landscape pursued by a cloud—see, it is here,
Passion and loneliness and all human pain
And these too living presences of wind and rain.
Say to the soul, Be still, in the quiet room
But what real ghosts come in or do not come?

## Evening Music

We enter this evening as we enter a quartet
Listening again for its particular note
The interval where all seems possible,
Order within time when action is suspended
And we are pure in heart, perfect in will.
We enter the evening whole and well-defended
But at the quick of self, intense detachment
That is a point of burning far from passion—
And this, we know, is what we always meant
And even love must learn it in some fashion,
To move like formal music through the heart,
To be achieved like some high difficult art.

We enter the evening as we enter a quartet
Listening again for its particular note
Which is your note, perhaps, your special gift,
A detached joy that flowers and makes bloom
The longest silence in the silent room—
And there would be no music if you left.

## Lullaby

If you deny
Love, ah then
Lie down, lie
With a ghost
And be well lost
To living men.

Pillow your head
On the bare floor
On the clean wood.
Stifle your tears
And years and fears
And close the door.

Someone will cry,
"Despair, despair,"
And your dry eye
Shiver for love
Though nothing move
And no one there.

Ghosts never die,
Nor can be hurt;
So lie down, lie
Alone, asleep,
But you'll not keep
Love out, lost heart.

Someone will knock
In the late dark
To sigh or mock,
A ghost be there
Upon the stair
Before the lark.

## Islands and Wells

In the private hour of night,
There are islands of light:
There is one, there is one
Ill in a great bed alone
Who without moving, moves
Like a delicate wind of caring
Over the earth, showering her loves
As a tree the leaves it has shed,
As a ship, world-faring,
Though anchored fast in her island-bed.

In the dry hour of the heart,
There are still wells in the desert:
There is one, there is one
To whom I once came down
From terrible Los Alamos of the bomb.
She opened wide the door.
She made me loving welcome,
And as we watched the setting sun, she spoke
Of suffering Europe, Asia. The world was near.
O human eyes! O deep imploring look!

In the dark night of the sense
When God is only felt as absence,
Prevenient grace is there
To tell us to endure
Since islands of pure light,
Since desert wells exist.
However dark our private night,
However far from Him, and how unsure,
There still is human love, moments of trust
That make us suddenly rich, however poor.

## Boy by the Waterfall

There by the waterfall
In the dappled green light
By the shaggy white coat
Of the steep fall in a second
Dream and reality were wedded.

The boy glimmered
Among the hollowed darkness of the rocks,
Shot through the shallow places laughing,
Stood in the sunlight, high up,
And like a god suspended in green air
He followed falling water and downstruck
Deep in the round pool; it trembled
With the force of that arrow in it.

What the mind pondered,
What the eye saw, met and
Were suddenly connected,
Opened the world within
As spirit sprang to sunlight:

Boy, did you meet Sabrina? Was she there?

To probe the secret dappled pools, to find her
Clothed in the curling sheepskin of the foam,
Under the green wave smiling, mind must be a diver,
It must follow the waters and take to the air.

Boy, dive again!
Suspended for a second in green air.
Perform and save us.
        Now there is only silence.

There is no connection any more between the pool
And the boy, between the actual image and the vision.
Dream and reality are parted.
        There is only, without end, division.

## Poets and the Rain

I will lie here alone and live your griefs.
Outside it rains and here the empty walls
And my own shoes empty beside the bed—
Strange tides pour through the river in my head.
I will lie here and answer outside calls:
I listen to the books and the beliefs.

I will receive you, passive and devout,
But soon must stand up in my shoes and shout.

Here the old man, hawk-cries and hawk-crest,
Looks out and taunts the world, sick of mankind,
Watching us tread like monkeys in the dance,
Riddled with doubt, hysteria and ignorance—
Old man, I hear your bird-scream on the wind.
I hear your voice shriller than all the rest.

Soon I must stand up in my shoes and dream
A hunting song to make the old hawk scream.

Here is the woman, frustrate and most pure,
Who builds a nest of blessings and there sits
Singing the lighted tree and the dark stone
(Many times to this woman I have come),
Who bids us meditate and use our wits
And we shall, with the help of love, endure—

Soon I must stand up in my shoes and weave
A simple song the birds would all believe.

Here the great girl, the violent and strong,
Who walks accompanied by dreams and visions,
Speaks with the blurred voice of a giant sleeping
And wakes to hear the foreign children weeping
And sees the crystal crack, the fierce divisions,
Asking deep questions in her difficult song.

Many times have I started up to answer them
And, standing, lost myself within her dream.

But winding through the labyrinth of mind
My song comes through and soon must speak aloud

I hear it in my ears, the roar of seas,
A swarming as of thousands of uprushing bees,
A sudden sweep of raindrops from the cloud,
I stand, rapt with delight, though deaf and blind,

And speak my poem now, leaves of a tree
Whose roots are hidden deep in mystery.

## Winter Grace

It is autumn again and our anxiety blows
With the wind, breaking the heart of the rose,
Petals and leaves fall down and everything goes.

All but the seed, all but the hard bright berry
And the bulbs we kneel on the earth to bury
And lay away with our anguish and our worry.

It is time we learned again the winter grace
To put the nerves to sleep in a dark place
And smooth the lines in the self-tortured face.

For we are at the end of our endurance nearly
And we shall have to die this winter surely,
For this is the end of more than a season clearly.

Now we shall have to be poor, to yield up all,
With the leaves wither, with the petals fall,
Now we shall have to die, once and for all.

Before the seed of faith so deep and still
Pushes up gently through the frozen will
And the joyless wake and learn to be joyful.

Before this buried love leaps up from sorrow
And doubt and violence and pity follow
To greet the radiant morning and the swallow.

# The Land of Silence
# (1950–1953)

# The First Autumn

*For E.M.S.*

Though in a little while
You will be dead again
After this first rehearsal
Since then and all the pain,
Still it's not death that spends
So tenderly this treasure
In leaf-rich golden winds,
But life in lavish measure.

October spends the aster,
Riches of purple, blue,
Lavender, white, that glow
In ragged starry cluster.
Then, when November comes,
Shaggy chrysanthemums,
Salmon-pink, saffron yellow,
All coppers bright and mellow,
Stand up against the frost
And never count the cost.

No, it's not death this year
Since then and all the pain.
It's life we harvest here
(Sun on the crimson vine).
The garden speaks your name.
We drink your joys like wine.

## The Sacred Wood

A charm of columns crowd
The tranquil glade;
No leaves to be seen,
The sudden rush of green
Makes of the air a cloud
Above the colonnade.

And this perspective breathes;
Unchanging, yet it grows.
The rich lives of the trees
Renew through centuries
Those columns and those wreaths
Through which the season flows.

The green rush comes and goes,
Light bursting through stained glass;
The coppers shine and fall
In the great airy hall,
But winter only shows
Structure more marvelous—

The columns in a choir
Define the empty air;
That leafy cloud has gone,
But only to bring on
This magic more severe,
The crucial form laid bare.

Oh, answer to a prayer
And to an old long hunger
This ancient fertile glade,
This living colonnade
Where form and content are
Not parted any longer!

## Summer Music

Summer is all a green air—
From the brilliant lawn, sopranos
Through murmuring hedges
Accompanied by some poplars;
In fields of wheat, surprises;
Through faraway pastures, flows
To the horizon's blues
In slow decrescendos.

Summer is all a green sound—
Rippling in the foreground
To that soft applause,
The foam of Queen Anne's lace.
Green, green in the ear
Is all we care to hear—
Until a field suddenly flashes
The singing with so sharp
A yellow that it crashes
Loud cymbals in the ear,
Minor has turned to major
As summer, lulling and so mild,
Goes golden-buttercup-wild.

## As Does New Hampshire

Could poetry or love by the same lucky chance
Make summer air vibrate with such a brilliance?
A landscape which says little—
Grave green hills diminishing to blue
Against the foreground of a long blond meadow,
While from the near pine elegantly falls
The nuthatch's neat syllable—
A landscape which says little,
But says this simple phrase so well
That it takes on forever the dimension
(Space, sound, silence, light and shade)
Of which a summer's happiness is made.
Only most daring love would care to mention
So much, so simply, and so charge each word
As does New Hampshire, mountain, meadow, bird.

## Transition

The zinnias, ocher, orange, chrome and amber,
Fade in their cornucopia of gold,
As all the summer turns toward September
And light in torrents flows through the room.

A wasp, determined, zigzags high then low,
Huting the bowl of rich unripened fruit,
Those purple plums clouded in powder blue,
Those pears, green-yellow with a rose highlight.

The zinnias stand so stiff they might be metal.
The wasp has come to rest on a green pear,
And as fierce light attacks the fruit and petal,
We sigh and feel the thunder in the air.

We are suspended between fruit and flower;
The dying, the unripe possess our day.
By what release of will, what saving power
To taste the fruit, to throw the flowers away?

## Villanelle for Fireworks

Across the darkness and the silent air
Where sleeping swans are lapped in their reflection
And the black lake's as empty as despair,

A brilliant burst of light, a shooting star
Explodes in clusters of soft swirling bloom
Across the darkness and the silent air.

But those flowers fall and vanish as we stare.
The swans have lurched in terror up and down,
And the black lake's as empty as despair.

There is no chance to mourn the melting flare,
For radiant fountains stream up and are gone
Across the darkness and the silent air.

Some little late moons float up slowly there,
A shower of glowworms in the darkening foam,
Then the black lake's as empty as despair.

So brightness falls away however rare;
We cannot give the falling star a home
Across the darkness and the silent air,
And the black lake's as empty as despair.

## Provence

The shadows are all black,
The sun intensely white,
And between this and that
No cloud or motion, but
Irradiating light.
Here silver olives shine
On terra cotta earth;
All scents are distilled—
Those fields of lavender
In the still, flaming air—
And sky's so primary blue
That half-tones disappear,
Each color its most true,
Each object its most clear.

Here death does not come
Through rot or through decay.
There is no mold nor rust;
The stone falls to dust,
The face crumbles away
On the round portal,
While the still, burning dome,
Primary blue, stays on,
Unchanging and impartial.

Here the rich Roman arch
And high-pillared tomb
Where the winds play alone
And where no legions march,
Stands in its triumph plain
To be the shepherd's wonder.
Only the antique power
Has been slowly refined
By the long years of light
To a more human splendor—
Yet here no tears can fall;
Here there is nothing at all
Between death and desire,
Between earth and fire.

## Journey by Train

Stretched across counties, countries, the train
Rushes faster than memory through the rain.
The rise of each hill is a musical phrase.
Listen to the rhythm of space, how it lies,
How it rolls, how it reaches, what unwinding relays
Of wood and meadow where the red cows graze
Come back again and again to closed eyes—
That garden, that pink farm, that village steeple,
And here and there the solitary people
Who stand arrested when express trains pass,
That stillness of an orchard in deep grass.

Yet landscapes flow like this toward a place,
A point in time and memory's own face.
So when the clamor stops, we really climb
Down to the earth, closing the curve of time,
Meeting those we have left, to those we meet
Bringing our whole life that has moved so fast,
And now is gathered up and here at last,
To unroll like a ribbon at their feet.

## Evening in France

France like the map of tenderness fell open
And green, green were the spreading arteries
Where every road was a leafy procession,
As poplar, maple, beech in lovely series
Opened the way to secret villages.
We were the wind, but even wind was slowed
As shadows made a river of the road.

We welcomed with a deep renewed devotion
Those gifts of evening wrapped in return:
The absent-minded cows moved in slow-motion,
The sleeping dog did not stir at our horn,
The haycart stopped us, bulging to the barn,
And red geraniums on each window sill
Warm like a handclasp, and as casual—

The immemorial boy fished in a stream
While the earth spun its way toward sleep;
Old women in the doorways sat to dream,
And at the fountain the old horse drank deep;
All animals and men were coming home.
We drove so fast it might have seemed like fleeing,
Yet all we knew was peace and its sweet flowing.

And as the moon rose and the mists rose too,
Still all we saw was radiance distilled
As we rushed down the tree-roads into blue.
We were the new world nourished by the old,
The wild natural heart gravely fulfilled
By France at its most pure that all men bless,
O human world, O map of tenderness!

## From All Our Journeys

I too have known the inward disturbance of exile,
The great peril of being at home nowhere,
The dispersed center, the dividing love,
Not here, nor there, leaping across ocean,
Turning, returning to each strong allegiance,
American, but with this difference, parting.

Wherever I could be was always parting,
Always anxiety, the sense of exile,
Settled in no place but a frightening nowhere.
And yet how strong was the transplanted love
Thrusting a fierce root into earth from ocean,
Seeking the nourishment of old allegiance.

Later the mind, Protean in allegiance,
Uprooted though it was, soon after parting
Did flower suddenly, astonished in its exile,
Became accustomed to a rootless nowhere,
Quick to bear fruit, but, Oh! my busy love
Needed those numbing journeys across ocean,

Made memory magic in the lapse of ocean,
Rehearsed the ancient cities till allegiance
Became eternal meeting and eternal parting,
A beautiful malaise between worlds of exile.
Would there be somewhere, someday, instead of nowhere,
A rock-bed for the elastic quickened love?

Can world-divisions heal a haunted love,
Now all earth is transformed to treacherous ocean?
What continent can hold our whole allegiance?
The whole world weeps, and there's an end of parting.
The tears of men are all the tears of exile.
Was it no place then, language, nightmare nowhere

But failure to recognize that Hell is nowhere
And becomes somewhere only through our love?
Insight by anguish fired leaps across ocean;

There are no formulas for this allegiance.
I've had to push on to the end of parting,
To emerge clumsily from inward exile,

Try to come home to a place beyond exile
Where love, that airy tree, is separate nowhere,
Greening impartial over every parting.

## Where Warriors Stood

We ask the peace of the spirit for each other,
A peace more difficult than mere not-strife,
The tired enemy beside his brother,
Possessing at last, but in sleep, his ardent life.

We ask something more ardous and deeper
Than calm suspension of the warring blood,
Than deathlikeness of an unconscious sleeper.
We ask a living peace where warriors stood.

Peace as we dream it is a wingèd strain:
Do you remember Victory on the stairs?
She who has lost her arms, poised and alone,
Still looks as if an unconquerable world were hers—

Though she stands broken and no ship behind her.

## Take Anguish for Companion

If the one certainty is suffering,
And if the only absolute is doubt,
From these alone belief must be wrung
Or else the bitter poverty found out:
Take anguish for companion and set out.

It leads us back to man himself, to sit
Down by his side whom we have killed and starved;—
Brother and sister, criminal and half-wit,
For each of us there is a place reserved,
To sit beside the one we have not served.

Wake as he dreams, dream as he wakes, to see
Man always at our side, starving and weeping,
Curved like a mother over his misery,
Huge and abandoned like a giant sleeping,
And we ourselves this creature we are keeping.

But if we dare to keep anguish companion,
We feel spring in our throats a living song,
See man leap from the rocks toward the sun,
Refuse to be imprisoned for too long,
His anger storming at the walls of wrong.

He is suddenly willing joy instead of power;
Shaken to the marrow by joy as by a flame,
Bending with mad delight toward a flower,
Secret and tender, violent, he came
Up from the darkness toward his haunting name.

He is the one who always sings and cries,
Believes, in spite of every proof, he will
Out of the darkness see with clearer eyes,
Conquer himself and learn to be an angel,
Who finds his only peace within the struggle.

For to be desperate is to discover strength.
We die of comfort and by conflict live
Who grow in this knowledge till at length
We find it good, find it belief enough
To be anguish alive, creating love.

# Innumerable Friend

*Ainsi du temple où seul l'ami entre, mais innombrable*
St. Exupéry

Let us forget these principalities,
Nations, governments, these mythical powers,
These real walls, these beleaguered cities;
We are theirs perhaps, but they are not ours.
We move, and must move always, one by one
Across the perilous frontiers alone,
And what we build be builded severally.
But who are "we" and is there still a "we"
Not lost uder the weight of history?
The poet, scientist and teacher know
How fast the seeds of hate and fear can grow,
What passions can take over peaceful nations,
What anguish lurk in the safe reservations.
Can we not start at the small roots again,
Build this "we" slowly, gently, one by one,
From each small center toward communion?
Reach over the frontier, stranger to stranger,
To find the only sure relief from danger?
Take the immense dangerous leap to understand,
Build an invisible bridge from mind to mind?
Swung out from letters or the briefest meeting
(Lives have been changed by a simple greeting)
Build an invisible bridge toward one person.
So the slow delicate process is begun,
The root of all relationship, and then
Learn that this stranger has become all men,
Flows through the open heart as a great host
Of all the human, solitary, lost.
His longing streams through the conventions
Of diplomats and their meager intentions,
Hunting for home like a great hungry wind.
He is the one, this our innumerable friend!

Let us forget these principalities, these powers;
We are theirs perhaps, but they are not ours.

Turn toward each other quietly and know
There are still bridges nations cannot overthrow.
And if we fight—if we must at the end—
These are the bridges we fight to defend.

## The Caged Bird

He was there in my room,
A wild bird in a cage,
But I was a guest and not for me
To open the gate and set him free
However great my gloom
And unrepenting rage.

But not to see and not to hear
Was difficult to try:
The small red bird burst into song
And sang so sweetly all day long
I knew his presence near
And his inquiring eye—

So we exchanged some words;
And then I scattered seed
And put fresh water in his pan
And cleaned the litter from the pen,
Wondering about caged birds,
What more this one might need.

But oh, when night came then
I started up in fear
At the fierce wing-beat of despair
Hurled at the bars, hurting the air,
And the heart wild within
As if a hawk were near.

The room was sealed and dark,
And that war all within
Where on the small cramped stage
The bird fought with his cage
And then lay beaten down,
Almost extinguished spark.

And I went back to bed,
Trembling, who nothing could,
As if this scene had grown so huge
It ripped apart all subterfuge,
And naked now as God,
I wept hot tears like blood.

## The Land of Silence

### 1

Time beats like a heart; we do not hear it
But we are nourished as by sleep after pain.
Death is so close to life that we can bear it.
The smallest veins drink time and breathe again.

### 2

Now I am here in the land of silence,
Of the near dove and the distant hills,
I know that the surface is the essence,
No stripping down to what is already bare,
No probing what is absolutely here.
This is the land of bones and violent dreaming
Where Heaven is woven in and out of Hell
And each not essence but actual and near.

More than for love we search for faith
Who in this high air must gasp for breath.

## Letter to an Indian Friend

Was it a long journey for you to begin
To grow peaceful green things,
To harvest well, to watch the sun
Go down, to find the ancient springs?
What human pain, what wild desire
Did you burn in the fire,
Long ago, Tilano?

What is the first step, Tilano,
Toward the wisdom of your feet,
Treading the dust or the snow
So quiet, so tender, so fleet?
I have come from far
To the warm sun and the shelter,
A long journey to reach here,
And now it is clear
That I do not know
The first step.

What is the first act, Tilano,
Toward the wisdom of your hands?
They plant the corn;
They bring in the lamp in the evening,
Wood for the fire, and each thing done
With rigorous love, with devotion.
It was a long journey to you and the sun,
And now it seems I clasp in your hand
A land of work and silence, a whole land.

What is the first prayer, Tilano?
To go into the forest
And be content to sit
For many days alone,
Not asking God to come,
Since He is present in the sun,
Simple and quiet in the tree and stone.
How many times have you watched the sun rise
That when I look into your eyes,
So old, so old and gay, I see there
That I have never learned the first prayer?

## Of Prayer

Straining the dark
For some answer,
Calling the strange dancer
With our formal prayers,
Hope for a private sign,
A secret world of grace,
We never meet your face,
Prince of the Imagination:
Not to our prayers have you been merciful.
Always the human faces
Open their eyes behind our lids
And all our questions become human questions,
So when we seek we do not find you
And you offer no suggestions.

But in that hour least expected
When we are most ourselves and not deflected
Even by remembrance of your name,
We stream down the paths of grace—
Hour of the poem or that hour
When two people war to the bone
And meet each other's skeleton.

Here desire is a tremendous flower;
Petals have steel in their growing,
Balance in power as the pillar
That supports arched leaves of stone.

It is a mistake, perhaps, to believe
That religion concerns you at all;
That is our own invention,
Longing for formal acceptance
To a formal invitation.
But yours to be the anarchist,
The thrust of growth,
And to be present only in the
Prayer that is creation,

In the life that is lived,
Love planted deeper than emotion,
Pure Idea that cannot break apart,
Creator of children or the work of art.

## The Tree

As it is brought in with its coat
Smelling of wilderness and yet not furry,
It still has an untamed look,
As if it might crash the ceiling
Or lie down in a corner and refuse
All welcome, an unwilling prisoner.
Small children and animals are wary
For fear it might break out or simply die,
Until it is time to set it up on end,
Sturdy, sweet-smelling, and so high
It makes a shelter and becomes a friend.

This is the moment to uncover
In boxes so light, what can they hold?—
From softest tissue to unwrap and gather
The apples of silver, the apples of gold.
Now gently deck the boughs, gently unfurl
The sprung branch that will wear
This lightest jewel in its pungent fur.
Is it real? Will it stay? Has it come
From so far, long ago, just to bloom
Just tonight, heart's desire, in this room?
The candles are lit, one by one, very slowly.
All gaze; all are silent; each child is holy.

The smallest, in pajamas, goes and lies
Under the boughs with dazzled open eyes,
And, as he looks up at the gaudy toys
They become strange and spiritual joys.
While the tree, stranger once from wilderness,
Is an angelic presence that can bless;
And all wound round now with the blazing truth,
The boy, the tree together are redeeming myth.

## A Light Left On

In the evening we came back
Into our yellow room,
For a moment taken aback
To find the light left on,
Falling on silent flowers,
Table, book, empty chair
While we had gone elsewhere,
Had been away for hours.

When we came home together
We found the inside weather.
All of our love unended
The quiet light demanded,
And we gave, in a look
At yellow walls and open book.
The deepest world we share
And do not talk about
But have to have, was there,
And by that light found out.

## Because What I Want Most Is Permanence

Because what I want most is permanence,
The long unwinding and continuous flow
Of subterranean rivers out of sense,
That nourish arid landscapes with their blue—
Poetry, prayer, or call it what you choose
That frees the complicated act of will
And makes the whole world both intense and still—
I set my mind to artful work and craft,
I set my heart on friendship, hard and fast
Against the wild inflaming wink of chance
And all sensations opened in a glance.
Oh blue Atlantis where the sailors dream
Their girls under the waves and in the foam—
I move another course. I'll not look down.

Because what I most want is permanence,
What I do best is bury fire now,
To bank the blaze within, and out of sense,
Where hidden fires and rivers burn and flow,
Create a world that is still and intense.
I come to you with only the straight gaze.
These are not hours of fire but years of praise,
The glass full to the brim, completely full,
But held in balance so no drop can spill.

## Song

This is the love I bring,
Absolute and nothing:
A tree but with no root,
A cloud heavy with fruit,
A wide stone stair
That leads nowhere
But to empty sky,
Ambiguous majesty.

This is the love I bear:
It is light as air,
Yet weighs like the earth;
It is water flowing,
Yet adamant as fire.
It is coming from going.
It is dying and growing.

A love so rare and hard
It cuts a diamond word
Upon the windowpane,
"Never, never again,
Never upon my breast,"
Having no time to bring
Having no place to rest,
Absolute and nothing.

## Leaves before the Wind

We have walked, looking at the actual trees:
The chestnut leaves wide-open like a hand,
The beech leaves bronzing under every breeze,
We have felt flowing through our knees
    As if we were the wind.

We have sat silent when two horses came,
Jangling their harness, to mow the long grass.
We have sat long and never found a name
For this suspension in the heart of flame
    That does not pass.

We have said nothing; we have parted often,
Not looking back, as if departure took
An absolute of will—once not again
(But this is each day's feat, as when
    The heart first shook).

Where fervor opens every instant so,
There is no instant that is not a curve,
And we are always coming as we go;
We lean toward the meeting that will show
    Love's very nerve.

And so exposed (O leaves before the wind!)
We bear this flowing fire, forever free,
And learn through devious paths to find
The whole, the center, and perhaps unbind
    The mystery

Where there are no roots, only fervent leaves,
Nourished on meditations and the air,
Where all that comes is also all that leaves,
And every hope compassionately lives
    Close to despair.

## In a Dry Land

We saw the rich leaves turning brown
And the small perfect grapes go sour,
Wizened by the devouring sun;
The brazen sky without a saving cloud
Burned on with an implacable blue fire,
And we were parched and dying like the vine
And only prayed to see the sun go down.

Until at last—after what nights of fever
When a full moon glittered the dead sky!—
We saw the weighted clouds come slowly over,
Purple, tumultuous against the brassy blue,
To burst upon the arid heights in thunder,
And our hearts like wild horses plunged,
Chaotic, trembling, in an agony of weather.

But when the rush of rain in mercy fell,
We knew the healing in our very bones,
And all the suffering landscape was made well:
Love rises green among the burning stones
Now that the little wizened grapes can swell.

## Prothalamion

How pure the hearts of lovers as they walk
Through the rich quiet fields
Where the stiff wheat grows heavy on the stalk,
And over barley and its paler golds
The air is bright—

Would touch it all, embrace, learn it by hand,
Plunging their faces into the thick grain,
To stroke as well as see the cow's soft flank,
To feel the beech trunk harsh under the palm,
And oh, to drink the light!

They do not even walk yet hand in hand,
But every sense is pricked alive so sharp
That life breathes through them from the burning land,
And they could use the wind itself for harp,
And pluck the vibrant green.

At first the whole world opens into sense:
They learn their love by looking at the wheat,
And there let fall all that was shy and tense
To walk the season slowly on propitious feet
And be all they have seen.

While all around them earth moves toward an end,
The gold turning to bronze, the barley tasseled,
Where the great sheaves will be stored up and bend
Their heads together in that rich wedding bed
All are about to enter.

The hearts of lovers as they walk, how pure;
How cool the wind upon the open palm
As they move on toward harvest, and so sure
Even this ripening has a marvelous calm
And a still center.

## Kinds of Wind

Wind in the stiff green wheat,
A thistly sound and sweet;
Wind in the barley tassels,
A heavy silk that rustles;
Wind seething in the leaves,
Waves on unbreaking waves.
The greening wind, the kind,
That comes from West or South,
All gently to unbind.

There is a fiercer blast,
That fills the whole sky's mouth,
That comes from North or East,
A god who can break through
The massive clouds to show
The coldest purest blue,
Or sometimes sudden snow.
Impersonal, immense,
It rushes toward silence.

Who feels this other wind,
Less gentle and less kind,
This cleansing ruthless will,
Learns the wind's heart is still,
Learns that pure love lies there
With grave wide open eyes,
The huge, the quiet skies,
The depth on depth of air.

## The Seas of Wheat

These dormant seas are lifted by the sun
Wave after sleeping wave in slow abandon
To burst against the blunt blue summer days
And brim the earth with their green folds
That will melt into blazing bronze and golds—
O ripening peace and rich repeated phrase!

Each year this presence fills the simplest need,
The seas, the golden seas, our daily bread.
We eat the miracle and hardly know we're blest.
What is lived here? a death and a birth
Between ourselves and the immense still earth?
Communion so intense it seems like rest.

We have watched all the changes come and go,
And all the ravaged fields asleep under the snow,
Seas without memory, withered and dead.
We have watched the black torrents of the rain
Rush through the furrows and that green again—
And all this was an image in the head,

But as we listen now to seas of wheat
All the deep riches grow articulate.
The word, the word that is incarnate sense
Bursts on the famished palate. What we eat
Is miracle, is love, immortal wheat.
O ripening peace and poetry's own presence!

## These Images Remain

### 1

Now that the evening gathers up the day,
All birds and treees and the delicious sum
Of scent and sound, of all instinctual play,
And hive-enclosed the bees' quiet hum,
I am so lonely for the commonplace,
The usual things of love, evenings and sleeps,
Multiple nights bringing the sound of wings,
Multiple mornings, every one for keeps,
I could almost despair of love that brings
So piercing a delight, so close to grief,
So full of absence that it learns to flourish
On a few hours, bearing a single leaf,
A single spring so great a tree to nourish;
On such a meager piece of earth, the root
Hugging what shallow bed to bear what fruit?

### 2

Even such fervor must seek out an end,
Magnificent and wasteful though it be,
Even such fervor granted to ascend
Long stairs of light in a pure majesty
Of longing and desire, impassioned progress
That has no end within reality
And so climbs on in careless loneliness
To look down on the sleeping human city,
Even such fervor must become so tired
It prays only a little place to creep;
A small real stone is more to be desired
Than all the world of light, an hour of sleep,
And those tears too expensive now that start
From radiant eyes and empty the whole heart.

### 3

So to release the soul, search out the soul
To make your open eyes suddenly see
As the last door slides back, that you are whole,

And you are here at last, and you are free
To stand like Aphrodite on her shell,
Wrapped in the wind, the net of nerves undone,
So piercingly alive and beautiful,
Her breasts are eyes. She opens in the sun
And sees herself reflected in the sand
When the great wave has left her naked there,
And looks at her own feet and her own hand
As on strange flowers and on her golden hair
As on some treasure given by the seas
To one who holds the earth between her knees.

### 4

The rose has opened and is all accomplished,
The inner violence of its growing done;
The petals, fashioned as the center wished,
Rest on the air in silent consummation,
Still held but all unfolded and resolved,
And still contained but with its falling near.
It is immense and quiet. It is solved.
Saint at the fire's center with no fear,
And like the saint detached from its own fall,
A rose of blood, a central seeing rose,
The legendary rose of the cathedral,
Transparent to the light, that does enclose,
Holy and wholly indivisible,
The heart of love and keeps it visible.

### 5

But parting is return, the coming home,
Parting in space and yet the dearest meeting;
Where most we seem to go, there most do come
And give each other an eternal greeting.
Love is restored to nobleness and peace,
Rooted in reason as abstract and pure
As the equation where all questions cease,
Love, with its deepest meaning to endure,
Endure and grow through all anxiety,
Until, when standing on the very quicksand,

Passion itself finds roots again in pity;
We take each other gently by the hand,
In deeper need demanding deeper union,
Parting become arrival and communion.

6

The stone withstands, but the chisel destroys
And out of deprivation the grave image
Slowly emerges and the sculptor's joys
Are made out of a self-denying rage—
Cut down and cast away, break to the core!
Whatever easy triumph falls in chips
And lies dispersed in waste upon the floor
He gladly yields for the sake of those lips,
That savage throat that opens the whole chest,
Tension so great between him and the stone,
It seems he carries vengeance in his wrist.
Now take the chisel and make for the bone!
Difficult love, you are the sculptor here,
The image you must wrest, great and severe.

7

What angel can I leave, gentle and stern,
What healing presence to be to you at last
The journey's end, the absolute return,
The future bringing gifts out of the past?
What angel can I take, gentle and pure,
To make of absence an open place of joy?
Now the perspective grows in depth, mature,
Untroubled love no parting can destroy,
As a great formal square where centuries
Only enrich the earlier design,
And cast a deeper shadow from the frieze
Of later leaves, and clarify the line.
The angel of these spaces, as we part,
Opens the sleeping city of the heart.

8

These images remain, these classic landscapes
That lie, immense and quiet, behind eyes

Enlarged by love to think only in shapes
That compass time and frame the changing skies,
Triumph of arch, of spire, triumph of trees,
The pure perspective, the poignant formal scene.
Pursued by time, still we were given these;
Even the flames of spring seemed frozen green,
Fountains suspended crystal on the air,
And every open square could make us glad.
Where we stood once, once free to stand and stare,
Imagination wanders like a god.
These images exist. They have not changed,
Though we are caught by time, by time estranged.

### 9

Here are the peaceful days we never knew.
Here are the leaves. Here are the silent flowers,
And you are reading poems while I sew.
The hours are light. We do not count the hours.
There is no need of words. Our lives will do,
Long long enough to learn all of our love,
While time, the river, flows gently below,
Having no false eternities to prove.
The night is full of unspent tenderness
And in its silences we rest apart.
There is no need of words with which to bless
The daily bread, the wine of the full heart.
Here are the peaceful days we cannot share.
Here is our peace at last, and we not there.

## Without the Violence

Without the violence, the major shift,
The shudder of the earth's foundations torn,
Without the great upheaval which could lift
That fiery core, it would not have been born,
And yet when chaos cooled, this land was here,
Absolute and austere—
Then, not before,
It snowed.
Later, by centuries and centuries,
The saving water flowed,
The grass arrived, dark little trees.
After a terrible and rending war,
This land took on its fearful peace,
After, and not before.

## Humpty Dumpty

Pain can make a whole winter bright,
Like fever, force us to live deep and hard,
Betrayal focus in a peculiar light
All we have ever dreamed or known or heard,
And from great shocks we do recover.
Like Wright's hotel we have been fashioned
To take earthquake and stand upright still.
Alive among the wreckage, we discover
Death or ruin is not less impassioned
Than we ourselves, and not less terrible,
Since we nicely absorb and can use them all.

It is the small shock, hardly noticed
At the time, the slight increase of gloom,
Daily attrition loosening the fist,
The empty mailbox in the afternoon,
The loss of memory, the gradual weakening
Of fiery will, defiant to exist,
That slowly undermines the solid walls,
Until the building that withstood an earthquake
Falls clumsily among the usual days.
Our last courage has been subtlty shaken:
When the cat dies, we are overtaken.

## Giant in the Garden

Innocence is the children's country, these
Full of wild pointless laughter, Christmas trees,
Birthdays gigantic when the self looms
Certain of greatness in the safer rooms,
Receives presents as its natural loot.
Innocence is not pure so much as pleased,
Always expectant, bright-eyed, self-enclosed,
But bursts into tears at a harsh word.
That self is lost when someone crashes through
To break the intact round I with a you.

The old really should not feel at home
In this fine country, safe as the womb.
The face without compassion, without guilt
Seems monstrous as the blank face of the pig
And children blush to discover the old baby
In grown-up language babbling secrets away.
It's even dangerous to play on alone
When all the children of your age have gone.
A willful giant looming in the garden
May like a mad dog one day go berserk
(Have you not heard the lewd and murderous bark?).

## Journey toward Poetry

First that beautiful mad exploration
Through a multiple legend of landscape
When all roads open and then close again
Behind a car that rushes toward escape,
The mind shot out across foreign borders
To visionary and abrupt disorders.
The hills unwind and wind up on a spool;
Rivers leap out of their beds and run;
The pink geranium standing on the wall
Rests there a second, still, and then breaks open
To show far off the huge blood-red cathedral
Looming like magic against a bright blue sky;
And marble graveyards fall into the sea.

After the mad beautiful racing is done,
To be still, to be silent, to stand by a window
Where time not motion changes light to shadow,
Is to be present at the birth of creation.
Now from the falling chaos of sensation
A single image possesses the whole soul:
The field of wheat, the telegraph pole.
From them the composed imagination reaches
Up and down to find its own frontier.
All landscapes crystallize and focus here—
And in the distance stand five copper beeches.

## Italian Garden

Where waterfalls in shining folds
Trouble the classic pools,
And always formal green enfolds
And frames the moving grays and golds—
Who breathes on stone, who makes the rules?

The dazzling spray of fountains
And sunlight flashing these
Silver and gold suspensions
Broken by leaves—
Who plays with these subtle and gay dimensions?

The cold triumphant stairs
Gentled by lichen and old moss
Rise up from watery lairs
Where light and shadow cross—
Who is received at these grave receptions?

Who past the long wall saunters on
Down the cool sheltered paths alone,
And at last climbs the lichened stair
To stand, astonished, in a bright blue air?

It's Poetry that's taken by surprise
In the most rigid of geometries.

## Letter from Chicago

*For Virginia Woolf*

Four years ago I met your death here,
Heard it where I had never been before
In a city of departures, streets of wind,
Soft plumes of smoke dissolving—
City of departures beside an aloof lake.
Here where you never were, they said,
"Virginia Woolf is dead."

The city died. I died in the city,
Witness of unreal tears, my own,
For experience involves time
And time was gone
The world arrested at the instant of death.
I wept wildly like a child
Who cannot give his present after all:
I met your death and did not recognize you.

Now you are dead four years
And there are no more private tears.
The city of departure is the city of arrival,
City of triumphant wind lifting people,
City of spring: yesterday I found you.
Wherever I looked was love.
Wherever I went I had presents in my hands.
Wherever I went I recognized you.

You are not, never to be again,
Never, never to be dead,
Never to be dead again in this city,
Never to be mourned again,
But to come back yearly,
Hourly, with the spring, with the wind,
Fresh as agony or resurrection;
A plume of smoke dissolving,
Remaking itself, never still,
Never static, never lost:
The place where time flows again.

I speak to you and meet my own life.
Is it to be poised as the lake beside the city,
Aloof, but given still to air and wind,
Detached from time, but given to the moment—
Is it to be a celebration always?

I send you love forward into the past.

## On a Winter Night

On a winter night
I sat alone
In a cold room,
Feeling old, strange
At the year's change,
In fire light.

Last fire of youth,
All brilliance burning,
And my year turning—
One dazzling rush,
Like a wild wish
Or blaze of truth.

First fire of age,
And the soft snow
Of ash below—
For the clean wood
The end was good;
For me, an image.

For then I saw
That fires, not I,
Burn down and die;
That flare of gold
Turns old, turns cold.
Not I. I grow.

Nor old, nor young,
The burning sprite
Of my delight,
A salamander
In fires of wonder,
Gives tongue, gives tongue!

# Now I Become Myself

Now I become myself. It's taken
Time, many years and places;
I have been dissolved and shaken,
Worn other people's faces,
Run madly, as if Time were there,
Terribly old, crying a warning,
"Hurry, you will be dead before—"
(What? Before you reach the morning?
Or the end of the poem is clear?
Or love safe in the walled city?)
Now to stand still, to be here,
Feel my own weight and density!
The black shadow on the paper
Is my hand; the shadow of a word
As thought shapes the shaper
Falls heavy on the page, is heard.
All fuses now, falls into place
From wish to action, word to silence,
My work, my love, my time, my face
Gathered into one intense
Gesture of growing like a plant.
As slowly as the ripening fruit
Fertile, detached, and always spent,
Falls but does not exhaust the root,
So all the poem is, can give,
Grows in me to become the song,
Made so and rooted so by love.
Now there is time and Time is young.
O, in this single hour I live
All of myself and do not move.
I, the pursued, who madly ran,
Stand still, stand still, and stop the sun!

# In Time Like Air
# (1953–1958)

# A Celebration for George Sarton

I never saw my father old;
I never saw my father cold.
His stride, staccato vital,
His talk struck from pure metal
Simple as gold, and all his learning
Only to light a passion's burning.
So, beaming like a lesser god,
He bounced upon the earth he trod,
And people marveled on the street
At this stout man's impetuous feet.

Loved donkeys, children, awkward ducks,
Loved to retell old simple jokes;
Lived in a world of innocence
Where loneliness could be intense;
Wrote letters until very late,
Found comfort in an orange cat—
Rufus and George exchanged no word,
But while George worked his Rufus purred
And neighbors looked up at his light,
Warmed by the scholar working late.

I never say my father passive;
He was electrically massive.
He never hurried, so he said,
And yet a fire burned in his head;
He worked as poets work, for love,
And gathered in a world alive,
While black and white above his door
Spoke Mystery, the avatar—
An Arabic inscription flowed
Like singing: "In the name of God."

And when he died, he died so swift
His death was like a final gift.
He went out when the tide was full,
Still undiminished, bountiful;
The scholar and the gentle soul,

The passion and the life were whole.
And now death's wake is only praise,
As when a neighbor writes and says:
"I did not know your father, but
His light was there. I miss the light."

## Dialogue

The teacher of logic said, "Reason."

The poet said, "Passion."

"Without logic, we muddle
And fail," said the teacher
Of reason.

     The poet said, "Fiddle!
What about Nature?"

"Has Nature no plan,
You poor fuddled creature?
You're a rational man,
Not an ape or an angel."

The poet said, "Nonsense!
I'm an angel, an ape,
And a creature of sense,
Not a brain in a box
That a mere jackanapes
With logic unlocks.
I'm total. I'm human.
It's you who are not."

"You sound like a woman."

The poet said, "Rot!
You're just a machine.
You can't write a poem.
You can't make a dream."

But the logical man
Said, "I'll stick to my reason."

(He said it with passion.)

## The Furies

One is large and lazy;
One is old and crazy;
One is young and witty;
One is a great beauty,
But all feed you the wind,
And each of them is blind.

How then to recognize
The hard unseeing eyes,
Or woman tell from ghost?
Human each is, almost—
That wild and glittering light—
Almost, and yet not quite.

Never look straight at one,
For then your self is gone.
The empty eyes give back
Your own most bitter lack,
And what they have to tell
Is your most secret Hell:

The old, the sad pursuit
Of the corrupting fruit,
The slightly tainted dish
Of the subconscious wish,
Fame, love, or merely pride
Exacerbate, provide.

Wrap you in glamor cold,
Warm you with fairy gold,
Till you grow fond and lazy,
Witty, perverse, and crazy,
And drink their health in wind,
And call the Furies kind.

## The Action of the Beautiful

I move through my world like a stranger
Where multiple images collide and fall,
Fragments of lakes, eyes—or a mirror.
How to include, make peace with them all?

Only your face (is this too illusion?)
So poised between silence and speech
Suggests that at the center of confusion
An inward music is just within reach.

Can so much be spoken by an eyelid,
Or the bent forehead so much light distill?
Here all is secret and yet nothing hid,
That tenderness, those deep reserves of will.

There is no future, past, only pure presence.
The moment of a glance is brimmed so full
It fuses consciousness to a new balance—
This is the action of the beautiful.

Lakes, mirrors, every broken radiance
Shine whole again in your reflective face,
And I, the stranger, centered in your presence,
Come home and walk into the heart of peace.

## On Being Given Time

Sometimes it seems to be the inmost land
All children still inhabit when alone.
They play the game of morning without end,
And only lunch can bring them, startled, home
Bearing in triumph a small speckled stone.

Yet even for them, too much dispersal scatters;
What complex form the simplest game may hold!
And all we know of time that really matters
We've learned from moving clouds and waters
Where we see form and motion lightly meld.

Not the clock's tick and its relentless bind
But the long ripple that opens out beyond
The duck as he swims down the tranquil pond,
Or when a wandering, falling leaf may find
And follow the formal downpath of the wind.

It is, perhaps, our most complex creation,
A lovely skill we spend a lifetime learning,
Something between the world of pure sensation
And the world of pure thought, a new relation,
As if we held in balance the globe turning.

Even a year's not long, yet moments are.
This moment, yours and mine, and always given,
When the leaf falls, the ripple opens far,
And we go where all animals and children are,
The world is open. Love can breathe again.

## The Metaphysical Garden

### I

It was late in September when you took me
To that amazing garden, hidden in the city,
Tranquil and complicated as an open hand,
There among green pleasances and descant of fountains,
Through walled paths and dappled loggias
Opening to distant trees,
We went conversing, smoking, often silent,
Our feet cool in sandals, nonchalant as the air.

It was at the end of September, warm for the season.
Nothing had fallen yet to bruise the grass.
Ripeness was all suspended,
The air aromatic and fresh over sun-drenched box.

Critical as Chinese philosophers,
We performed the garden by easy stages:
Should we move toward shade or toward sunlight,
The closed dark pool or the panoplied fountain?
Clearly each path had a metaphysical meaning,
Those rustic steps, that marble balustrade.
It was late in September when time,
Time that is not ours,
Hid itself away.

### II

Our first arrival was a square room,
Brilliant parquet of clover
Designed as a stage for the trees
And their subtle conversations,
Diapason of faintly stirring leaves;
The fountains, heard not seen,
Made silence crepitant aand watery.
And here it seemed we were part of a discourse
On the ancient themes,
Perspective and enclosure,
Desire raised and fulfilled
To this complex alive composure.

It was there that your voice,
Harsh and aloof,
Mixed with the cry of a bird
As a cardinal flashed through the willow
And suddenly screamed.

### III

We climbed lightly
Through a small steep orchard
To a bastion of branches.
Must we penetrate, force passage
At the top of the hill?
No airy place, no view?

What we found was a grave high room,
Lonely, enclosed in acacias,
Its center a double pool
Where ivy crept and crowded
And water lilies slept, going to seed.
We had not after all expected
A place so perfectly round.
We sat on a stone bench like statues.
Nothing moved.

Nothing moved for a long season.
From high in the sunlight then
A single leaf fell slowly,
And we watched it fall.
So passionate was the place, so still,
This light leaf falling from air to grass
Was monumental. It held
The exact weight of a tremendous word.

### IV

How gentle and relieving
Then to emerge, climb down
From that intense enclosure
High on the hill
To the large view we had imagined

Through all the devious paths,
The orchards, loggias,
The long boxed-in perspectives.

Now it was here,
The weight of the trees flung back,
The undulating ample slopes,
The whole shape of the land
Made clear in the golden light.
In the foreground tawny dogwood
Thick with vermilion berries, showed
Brilliantly sharp.
We could read each leaf.

We had to climb down
To get to contemplatiton
On this scale, large, airy, remote.
We sat on a homely wooden bench
And watched a solitary gardener pass
With his pruning hook.
Indeed it was coming home
To an unbroken sunlit peace of knowing.

## Where Dream Begins

Strip off kindness,
Strip off shelter,
Stripped down, friendless,
Nor pride, nor warm shoes,
Nor any covering
A cold man might use
When there is no sun,
When heart is gone.

Without coat or cape,
Shoestring or doorlatch,
Or one cosy hope,
Stripped of odds and ends,
Even at last of love,
Where the world ends,
Go rich in poverty,
Go rich in poetry.

This nothingness
Is plenitude,
Honeycomb wilderness
Where the wild hare runs,
Wind in the torn seams,
Where rise buried suns,
Where darkness begins.
Here dream begins.

## Lament for Toby, a French Poodle

The great Toby is dead,
Courteous and discreet,
He of the noble head,
Remote and tragic air,
He of the trim black feet—
He's gone. He is nowhere.

Yet famous in New Hampshire
As one who fought and killed—
Dog-bane and dog-despair—
That prey that all resign,
The terrible and quilled,
Heraldic porcupine.

He will become a legend,
Black coat and royal nature,
So wounded he was blind,
As on a painted shield
Some lost heroic creature
Who fought and would not yield.

If we were brave as he,
Who'd ask to be wise?
We shall remember Toby:
When human courage fails,
Be dogged in just cause
As he before the quills.

# Green Song

Here where nothing passes,
Where centuries have stayed
Alive under the grasses,
Gently the heart is laid.

Oh, breathe these meadows in
Till you are filled with green,
A drunkard of the scene
Your dreams will wander in.

Then set the eyes to graze,
Set urban eyes to browse
These rich, brief summer days
Among the trees and cows.

And sleep away all care,
Lay rushing time to rest,
And rise up light as air,
Green-fed and meadow-blessed.

## These Were Her Nightly Journeys

*O joie—mon abîme parle. J'ai retourné vers la lumière ma
dernière profondeur!*

Nietzsche

These were her nightly journeys made alone,
The prisoner of seas which cannot drown,
Forced to descend the vertical
Plunges of dream.
Though all day long she knew no fear would come
And freely walked (who once in dreams had flown),
At night, she fell.
Burdens returned to magnetize the bone,
And in her helpless sleep she was hurled down.

Waters were heavy round her; she was bound
To heaviness of falling, falling with no end,
Imprisoned plunge
Sucked by dense air;
Or, worse, vertiginous oceans with no floor.
She fell and must keep falling, nearly drowned,
Yet cling to the lunge,
Gasp for more breath, for falling must extend:
She would be dead if once she touched the ground.

Yet once on the voyage through the night, she was
Given (but how? but why?) the means of choice:
She might choose to ascend
The falling dream,
By some angelic power without a name
Reverse the motion, plunge into upwardness,
Know height without an end,
Density melt to air, silence yield a voice—
Within her fall she felt the pull of Grace.

Through the descending motion a strong thrust
Strengthened her upward against the fluid wall—
So splitting-fierce a tension,
Psychic strain,
She turned weak, dizzy for downwardness again,
But was upheld, drawn upward, upward to free air,

Felt herself all ascension,
And floated through blue spaces over all,
Needing no walls, suspended on pure trust.

And when she came back to cool daylight, found
That she brought with her from that mystic sleep
The saving true event,
The image raised
In glass at a great height where angels blazed,
And there, at Chartres, as the sun made its round,
One crimson angel sent
A bolt down to her human world to keep,
A bolt that struck her knees back to the ground,

A bolt that raised her heart to blazing height
And made the vertical the very thrust of hope,
And found its path at last
(Slow work of Grace)
Into the texture of the nightmare place,
Shot through the falling dream, entered her night,
Lifted her past
The watery dark burdens, the descending slope
Until she was both grounded and in flight.

## The Olive Grove

Here in the olive grove,
Under the cobalt dome,
The ancient spirits move
And light comes home,

And nests in silvery leaves.
It makes each branch a cloud,
And comes and goes, and weaves
Aerial song aloud.

Here every branch is gifted
With spiritual fruit
And every leaf is lifted
To brightness from the root.

Where the terrestrial plane
Meets vision and desire,
The silver and the green
Are strung on a great lyre,

And leafy seraphim
The sun and shade among
Turn each grove to a hymn;
Whole hillsides are in song.

Silvery, shadowy now
The fruit over our head,
Who lie and hardly know
which is light, which is bread.

## Mediterranean

Here is the ample place,
Hid in the sacred wood,
Where the intense young face
Meets the calm antique god,

Light flowing through the vine
Where air and earth are one;
Here are the sovereign wine,
The dark bread, the gold sun.

Distill all that's concrete
And make of it a prayer:
Air is the fig you eat;
The wine you drink is air.

This is the calm god's will,
And what he knows you know.
Lie under the terraced wall
And let the anguish go.

Let fall the torturing dream
Where the slow oxen move.
All things are what they seem
Here in the sacred grove.

## At Muzot

In this land, Rilke's country if you will,
Nothing is closed or intact.
The mountains open out an airy world and spill
Height as an ethos. We live in the vertical.
Angels, often invoked, become a fact.

And they have names, Cloud, Stone, Sun, Vine,
But the names are interchangeable.
All meld together in making the same flowing design;
We drink conjunction in the mingled wine.
The journey is infinite and it is immobile.

This is what he found after all the busy wanderings,
This childhood dream of a lonely tower
Set in a mountain-meadow world where the air sings
And the names are interchangeable of cloud and flower.
This is what he found: the grass full of springs.

A sacramental earth; reality both stalked
and made the vision clear.
And here the living waters sprang up where he walked.
It was the clouds and not himself who talked.
Was he the ghost who felt himself so near?

At Muzot he stood at last at the intersection
Of God and self (nothing is closed).
The voice he heard came from dissolving stone.
Even the mountains ascended and were gone,
And he himself stood naked and disclosed.

# To the North

We have come back to the cold North,
Come home after the passionate going forth,
After the olive groves, the Alpine meadow,
The purple seas under a mountain shadow,
The rich and crumbling ruins in the hills
Those storms of light in the psychic cathedrals.
After the passionate summer going forth,
We have come back to the cold North.

We have come at the year's turning,
Before the leaves fall, when the leaves are burning,
Before the apples, the late roses, fall,
When all is empty and yet bountiful.
We have cried "Beauty, Beauty!" up and down,
But that restless pursuit is overthrown,
And Beauty turned to ashes in the mouth,
Consumed by the consuming South.

Oh splendid was that spendthrift living,
The quick growth in the South, the overgiving,
But ripeness tumbles swiftly into ruin
And death is there under that awful sun,
The fig bursting with sweetness, the grape broken,
And every word too heavy that is spoken—
And we come back now, silenced, to this earth
To bind up selfhood in the North.

## After Four Years

How to lay down her death,
Bring her back living
Into the open heart, the overgrieving,
Bury once and for all the starving breath
And lay down her death?

Not on love's breast
Lay down this heavy prize
And close at last the open, the gray eyes
Of her who in my woe can find no rest—
Not on love's breast.

And not in solitude
Lay the long burden down,
For she is there awake when I'm alone,
Who cannot sleep, yet sorely, sorely would—
Oh, not in solitude!

Now everywhere I'm blind;
On the far journeys
Toward the magical old trees and cities
It's the same rooted sorrow that I find,
And everywhere I'm blind.

Is there a human prayer
That might unknot prolonged
Unnatural grief, grief that has surely wronged
Her very radiant presence in the air,
Is there a human prayer?

It is poor love, I know,
Mother and marvelous friend,
Over that final poverty to bend
And not remember all the rich life too:
It is poor love, I know.

"Rich love, come in,
Come home, my treasure.
All that you were and that no word can measure
Melt itself through me like a healing balm,
Rich love, come home."

And here lay down at last
Her long hard death,
And let her be in joy, be ash, not breath,
And let her gently go into the past,
Dear world, to rest at last.

## Somersault

Not to rebel against what pulls us down,
The private burdens each of us could name
That weigh heavily in the blood and bone
So that we stumble, clumsy half the time
Unable to love well or love at all!
Who knows the full weight that another bears,
What obscure densities sustains alone,
To burst fearfully through what self-locked doors?
So heavy is our walk with what we feel,
And cannot tell, and cannot ever tell.

Oh, to have the lightness, the savoir faire
Of a tightrope walker, his quicksilver tread
As he runs softly over the taut steel thread;
Sharp as a knife blade cutting walls of air,
He's pitted against weights we cannot see,
All tension balanced, though we see him only
A rapture of grace and skill, focused and lonely.

Is it a question of discipline or grace?
The steel trap of the will or some slight shift
Within an opened consciousness?
The tightrope walker juggles weights, to lift
Himself up on the stress, and, airy master
Of his own loss, he springs from heaviness.
But we, stumbling our way, how learn such poise,
The perfect balance of all griefs and joys?
Burdened by love, how learn the light release
That, out of stress, can somersault to peace?

## The Frog, that Naked Creature

The frog, that naked creature,
Arouses immediate pity;
He does not burst except in fables, but
He looks as if he might,
So violent his anxiety,
So exposed his nature.
His brilliant eyes look wildly out
As if the pulse were leaping from his throat.

We feel his being more, now
We have grown so vulnerable,
Have become so wholly exposed with the years
To primeval powers;
These storms are often terrible,
Followed by sudden snow.
It is alarming to feel the soul
Leap to the surface and find no sheltering wall.

Is this growth, we wonder?
But it makes us tremble,
Because we are not able to conceal
The rage, the fear we feel,
Nor able to dissemble
Those claps of thunder
When we are seized and shaken beyond our will
By the secret demon or the secret angel.

To show the very pulse
Of thought alive,
Transparent as the frog whose every mood
Glows through his cold red blood—
For whom we grieve
Because he has no walls—
Giving up pride, to endure shame and pity,
Is this a valid choice, choice of maturity?

## The Phoenix

It is time the big bird with the angry neck,
We have cajoled and cursed,
Went home to die, or whatever he must do
When his heart would burst.

For his wild desire pulses over our heads
And opens the secret night,
Passage of wings that madden without release,
When the phoenix is in flight.

Let him go, stretching his long legs, clumsy
On this harsh ground. Let him flee
To the soft black marshes he remembers
Or the gentle mother tree.

Let him go. He has shaken the house at night;
His wings have clouded our dream,
And there is no peace for his lost cry at daybreak
And at night his terrible scream.

He flames through the morning yet he never sings;
He only makes that strange lost cry.
He is angry all the time. Let him find his tree
And make his nest and die.

Though he is God's own angel in disguise,
We cannot bear another angry word,
Nor look into those cold and jeweled eyes,
O pitiless strange bird!

Will he come back, will he come back all shining
From his dark death, to bring
The true message, the gentle, that all his torment
Was desperate to sing?

Or—what if it were not he at all, not he
Who must consume himself to be reborn,
But we ourselves, who drove an angel from us
Because our hearts were torn?

## In Time Like Air

Consider the mysterious salt:
In water it must disappear.
It has no self. It knows no fault.
Not even sight may apprehend it.
No one may gather it or spend it.
It is dissolved and everywhere.

But, out of water into air,
It must resolve into a presence,
Precise and tangible and here.
Faultlessly pure, faultlessly white,
It crystallizes in our sight
And has defined itself to essence.

What element dissolves the soul
So it may be both found and lost,
In what suspended as a whole?
What is the element so blest
That there identity can rest
As salt in the clear water cast?

Love, in its early transformation,
And only love, may so design it
That the self flows in pure sensation,
Is all dissolved, and found at last
Without a future or a past,
And a whole life suspended in it.

The faultless crystal of detachment
Comes after, cannot be created
Without the first intense attachment.
Even the saints achieve this slowly;
For us, more human and less holy,
In time like air is essence stated.

## Nativity

*Piero della Francesca*

O cruel cloudless space,
And pale bare ground where the poor infant lies!
Why do we feel restored
As in a sacramental place?
Here Mystery is artifice,
And here a vision of such peace is stored,
Healing flows from it through our eyes.

Comfort and joy are near,
Not as we know them in the usual ways,
Personal and expected,
But utterly distilled and spare
Like a cool breath upon the air.
Emotion, it would seem, has been rejected
For a clear geometric praise.

Even the angels' stance
Is architectural in form:
They tell no story.
We see on each grave countenance,
Withheld as in a formal dance,
The awful joy, the serene glory:
It is the inscape keeps us warm.

Poised as a monument,
Thought rests, and in these balanced spaces
Images meditate;
Whatever Piero meant,
The strange impersonal does not relent:
Here is love, naked, lying in great state
On the bare ground, as in all human faces.

## Annunciation

Here in two ways perspective leads us on
From matter and from moment: we explore
A flight of arches diminished one by one
Above converging lines upon the floor;
They bring us, captivated, to an open door.

From everything that might trouble the mind
This narrowing path is drawn to set us free,
Sends us to Heaven curiously designed—
We cannot help but go there when we see
The hill, the cool blue air, the pointed tree.

The matter and the moment are forgotten
But they are always there, still taking place.
The angel tells of Love to be begotten,
And we, who have been running free in space,
Come back refreshed, to meet it face to face.

## All Souls

Did someone say that there would be an end,
An end, Oh, an end, to love and mourning?
Such voices speak when sleep and waking blend,
The cold bleak voices of the early morning
When all the birds are dumb in dark November—
Remember and forget, forget, remember.

After the false night, warm true voices, wake!
Voice of the dead that touches the cold living,
Through the pale sunlight once more gravely speak.
Tell me again, while the last leaves are falling:
"Dear child, what has been once so interwoven
Cannot be raveled, nor the gift ungiven."

Now the dead move through all of us still glowing,
Mother and child, lover and lover mated,
Are wound and bound together and enflowing.
What has been plaited cannot be unplaited—
Only the strands grow richer with each loss
And memory makes kings and queens of us.

Dark into light, light into darkness, spin.
When all the birds have flown to some real haven,
We who find shelter in the warmth within,
Listen, and feel new-cherished, new-forgiven,
As the lost human voices speak through us and blend
Our complex love, our mourning without end.

## Lifting Stone

*A painting by Katharine Sturgis*

This is an ancient scene: we stand and stare
As hills are excavated and then lifted;
Swung on the cable's perpendicular,
The load is pivotal to earth and air,
A feather-balance, and so delicate
The stone floats up as if it had no weight.

Below a solitary figure stands
To gentle the long bundle from its bed;
Athens and Troy are leaning from his hands;
The Roman arch, then perilous Chartes ascends
Out of the empty spacious world where he
Nudges rich burdens toward history.

Who, with his own machineries of skill,
Has not dreamed often of this very place?
Painter and poet lift the buried hill
To build a pyramid or clean bright wall,
And the great spires that sleep in this quarry
Are excavated toward the clouds they marry.

What soars is always buried deep for ages,
Gently explored in the hill's dark mind,
Prized, hewn in slow thoughtful stages,
Then floated on these airy equipages,
Watched by a figure standing there alone.
Whose work, humble and hard, is lifting stone.

## Binding the Dragon

"The dragon's Proteus. He must be fought,
And fighting dragons is my holy joy,"
The poet says, although he may look caught
And blood is spurting from one eye.

"Sublimate," says the cautious analyst.
The poet answers, "Let him do it first.
Look, I have got this dragon in my fist.
I'll hold him here until he dies of thirst."

But suddenly the dragon flows away.
The dragon is a river: you can't do it,
Hold up a river in your hands all day.
"And what is sublimation?" asks the poet.

"Is it to translate water into fire?
Is it to follow birds along the air?
Is it to be the master of desire,
Or ride a cycle with no handlebar?

Gentle a dragon to lie quiet there,
Beautiful in his power but asleep,
Image of dragon resting on the air?"
The poet asked, and then began to weep.

He did not want the dragon to be caught.
He wanted it alive and in his fist.
For who would kill the god with whom he fought?
And so he wept and cursed the analyst.

## The Fall

Measure force of tension
By its end,
From the strained suspension
Supported, spanned
On taut skies of will,
Slack now, sudden, and
Heavily we fall.

Mortal is the tug
Of gravity,
And the heart-huge hug
That pulls down sky.
Dark clouds enfold us
And then fall away—
Nothing to hold us.

Toward what landing
Do we fast-fall
In this strange unhanding
And release of will,
Heavy bodies now
(Sky, farewell!)
To what earth below?

Toward a new land,
But from where or why
Never understand,
Who you are or I,
By what perils, charms
Come by chance to lie
In each other's arms.

## The Other Place

We are suddenly there
In the other place;
After the long war
Discover peace:
I touch your face.

The open palm
Marries your bone,
Beyond all things calm
Finds crucial form,
Lies still as stone.

Flesh is made whole
That held us caught.
There is no wall.
We lie where we fought
Lost in pure thought.

Our truth is here
In this still pond
Where without fear
The soul's alive beyond
What we can understand.

# Definition

This fullness that is emptiness,
This hunger that is food;
This union, solitariness,
This wild air, this warm blood;
This poverty, and rich sensation,
This haste, this slow growing,
True marriage, separation,
All-knowing that is not-knowing;
Late fulfillment, early death,
This huge passion, this small breath.

## Forethought

What is left at the end?
Shape of a mouth or a hand,
Something not understood
That they must understand?
Nothing left at the end,
Not a breath or a touch:
These lovers loved so much
All was consumed. Desire
Burned itself in the fire.
When they arise estranged,
When nothing's left to burn,
And coldness at the bone,
No, they will not return.
They will stand up full-grown,
And love itself be changed
To walk the earth alone.

## A Pair of Hands

Indeed I loved these hands and knew them well—
Nervous, expressive, holding a Chinese pink,
A child, a book always withdrawn and still
As if they had it in their power to think:
Hands that the Flemish masters have explored,
Who gave delicate strength and mystic grace
To contemplative men, to women most adored
As if to give the inmost heart a face—
Indeed I learned to love these secret hands
Before I found them here, open to mine,
And clasped the mystery no one understands,
Read reverence in their fivefold design,
Where animals and children may be healed
And in the slightest gesture Love revealed.

## My Father's Death

After the laboring birth, the clean stripped hull
Glides down the ways and is gently set free,
The landlocked, launched; the cramped made bountiful—
Oh, grave great moment when ships take the sea!
Alone now in my life, no longer child,
This hour and its flood of mystery,
Where death and love are wholly reconciled,
Launches the ship of all my history.
Accomplished now is the last struggling birth,
I have slipped out from the embracing shore
Nor look for comfort to maternal earth.
I shall not be a daughter any more,
But through this final parting, all stripped down,
Launched on the tide of love, go out full grown.

## The Light Years

Locked to each other's heart, floating at rest,
These lovers stream the night like constellations;
The throat a flaming pillar and the breast
A Milky Way, these shining convocations
In one brief hour reverse the elements,
And bring down to the earth the starry sky;
A single touch halos the shadowy hands,
And brilliant as the Pleiades they lie,
Floating like milkweed on the winter cold,
Resting as gently on the weightless air;
They will not ever change, will not grow old,
Who have flown out of time and wander there
In radiance that's counted in light-years—
Until dawn tilts earth back; a tree appears.

## Spring Day

Beautiful is this day that brings us home
From our domain of cold and winter bower,
From iron earth to trees in tassely flower,
And gentle airs, and the soft-springing loam.

Offhand and royal, we are the carefree lords
Of these sumptuous rooms where light flows green,
These corridors of air, these feathery swards
Under a sky-blue ceiling, high and clean.

We lie on an enormous grassy bed
Sheltered as princes under the mothering air,
Where the anemone shines like a star,
And rivers flow through veined leaves overhead;

And hold each other close in the green chance,
Hold each other against time and waste,
Come home here in a spring that is only once
And watch how the birds are swift, yet without haste.

At last we inhabit the dream, are really floating
As princes of the hour, while these green palaces
Glide into summer, where we too are going
With all the birds, and leaves, and all the kisses.

# By Moonlight

We are true lovers without hope
Whose hearts are locked to time,
So lie with me on the grassy sward
On the cool black-shadowed slope,
For we'll not sleep in a close warm room:
Whatever we are moving toward
An ample bed's not our reward
Who are mad with the moon.

Wherever passionate love is leading
We'll be discovering alone,
So little hope it can endure,
So wild, so deep, so dark the needing
That, even fastened bone to bone,
We'll not have lasting peace, that's sure,
Nor any haven from despair
Who love by light of moon.

So come, though we shall never rest
In any house to call our own,
By any hearth we light and tend,
Lie here upon the cold earth's breast
And lean your length hard on the stone:
Hearts break and they may also mend
But here until the certain end,
Wed me by light of moon.

Now the great open sky is ours
And the long light across the loam,
And we, gigantic hearts of dust,
Lie open like night-blooming flowers.
The homeless moon is our bright home,
And we shine too because we must,
Oh magic that we cannot trust,
The lovely changing moon!

## Reflections in a Double Mirror

There is anxiety hot in the throat,
The dark wood where even lovers get lost,
The ax held loosely, dangerous in the hand
That might slip, those cloudy dreams of threat.
There is always ahead some next, more awful test,
Or again the bog, indifference, dragging quicksand;
There is the never-ending battle with
The unforgiven, unforgiving self for truth.
It may all prove untenable for lack of hope,
Something we cannot deal with or escape—

These are the things we lie awake to ponder.

There is in each of us a healing mother;
There is the hand cradling the ax, breaking
Dead wood down, held lightly with clean grace;
There is the help we can give each other,
And every morning, light at our first waking
As if each day a blessing did take place.
Despite all fumbles, bungling, we endure,
Manage to go on building the hard inner core,
A free self that might harbor faithful love.
There is more in us than we have learned to give.

These are the things we lie awake to ponder.

## Death and the Lovers

For a time it is part of the machinery
Of feeling, one of the several counters
In the game: romantic love encounters
Death, and death is romantic scenery,
A stage device for deepening the view,
Papier-mâché of course. It can't be true.

Later it will become the central fact,
Not in imagination's realm at all,
But reckoned with, an implacable fall,
And to be felt under every wish or act—
The kiss, straight from the terrible heart
That will not beat forever, must, does hurt.

Death becomes real, and love is forced to grow.
These lovers do not turn away to weep,
But hold carefully all they have to keep,
And stare long at all they have to know.
When every gesture is made upon a quicksand,
Touch must be absolute and firm the hand.

Not by not seeing, but by seeing through:
With fresh clear eyes they search out each other,
As once the infant searched to find the mother,
And make a strong one out of a frail two.
These lovers, who have learned to reckon death,
Are gravely married on the moment's breath.

# Cloud, Stone, Sun, Vine
# (1958–1961)

# A Divorce of Lovers

## 1

Now these two warring halves are to be parted,
And the long struggle to anneal, come through
To where divided love could grow whole-hearted,
Is given over. Now we are cut in two.
Never will you and I meet face to face,
Never again, you say, upon this ground;
So our last battle was a special grace—
An ether to anaesthetize the wound.
When we are conscious, we shall understand
Better, perhaps, just how it can be done—
How surgeons crack apart the tight-clasped hand,
What scalpel can unknot love at the bone.
The surgeon's name is Reason. We shall see
How Reason operates on Poetry.

## 2

I shall not see the end of this unweaving.
I shall lie dead in any narrow ditch
Before they are unwoven, love and grieving,
And our lives separated stitch by stitch.
I shall be dead before this task is done,
Not for a moment give you your cool head.
Say we had twenty years and now have none—
Are you Old Fate itself to snap the thread,
And to cut both your life and mine in half
Before the whole design is written clear?
This tapestry will not unweave itself,
Nor I spend what is left of me to tear
Your bright thread out: let unfulfilled design
Stand as your tragic epitaph, and mine.

## 3

One death's true death, and that is—not to care.
We do not die of feeling: even the extreme
Great arc of tension we had learned to bear.

I woke once out of a disturbing dream:
I could not reach you. You were lost and cold.
And the worst was I did not even mind,
Distant myself, and tired like the old—
But then you woke and tender love was kind.
Now you condemn us to wake up alone
Without a human breast on which to lie
Until we sleep at last against a stone,
Still let me say I live and shall not die:
When you kill love and reason mystery,
You have condemned yourself to death, not me.


### 4

Did you achieve this with a simple word?
Chase out the furies and the plagues of passion,
Cut through the shapes of conscience with your sword
And make your peace in such a ruthless fashion?
I wonder what the weapon really was,
It is so windless here, so very still,
And we move through our palaces of glass
As freezing cold as if this world were Hell.
My guess is that the weapon's name was Pride.
It is a word the Furies understand;
Their ghosts are gathering on every side,
And they will raise the hair upon your hand.
For who can punish ghosts or give them warning?
They will be there at night, and in the morning.


### 5

What price serenity these cruel days?
Your silence and ungiving, my small cries,
Followed by hours when I can lift some praise
And make the wound sing as in Paradise.
What price the poise you ask for, the unharried?
Four rooted years torn up without a qualm,
A past not dead perhaps, but quickly buried:
On one side anguish, on the other calm,
Both terrible because deprived of hope
Like living eyes still open in a grave.
And we shall lunch, you say, that is our scope.

Between what we have lost and still might save
Lies, very quiet, what was once too human,
And lovely, and beloved, a living woman.

### 6

Dear fellow-sufferer, dear cruelty,
"I feel so married to you," once you said,
And it is you who now unmarry me.
I wish I could hold fast your tired head,
Or bind up all the wounds that we have made,
Say that I never hurt, you never saddened,
Say we were good and peaceful, undismayed—
The truth is that we always wounded, maddened,
Tore every joy out of such pain, it is
No wonder that the battle nearly killed.
From such inhuman ways you wish to save us:
Oh, is it better now, all anguish stilled?
Tell me what sovereign remedy you found
To call this better, this one mortal wound?

### 7

Your greatness withers when it shuts out grief
And must assert itself through the denying
Of what was lately sap and the green leaf,
And this new stance resembles only dying.
Castrati have pure voices, as we know;
But the mature, who mutilate by choice,
Who cut the heart out so that they may grow,
What sweetness flows from such a tortured voice?
So you would gather in and cherish power,
"Today I have grown old," is your decree;
You cut down passion like a summer flower,
And chill the ripening season's warmth in me,
Whose strength was wiser when you could enfold
Another in your arms against the cold.

### 8

Now we have lost the heartways and the word,
Our senses blinded, our five wits too numb,

Like planes that circle, or a blundering bird
That cannot chart the clouded skies for home.
Now rocked and hurtled through the empty spaces,
We hang upon the hope that some thin radar
May light from deep within our darkened faces,
And tell us what to do, and where we are;
Focus the awful blurring of the dream,
And give some destination to the heart.
What can it tell us, that deep inward beam,
How write a new course on this troubled chart?
Will this lost journey never have an end
Nor the skies open so that love may land?

### 9

What if a homing pigeon lost its home,
Were wrenched out of the orbit of sensation,
Its instinct killed, what would it then become?
A haunted traveler with no destination,
Circling the air above strange roosts to climb
Upward again, more fearful, more harassed,
The gentle voice repeating all the time
The phrases that had meaning in the past,
"Where is my true love, O where is my nest?
Where can I shut this terrible bright eye
And put my head under a wing to rest?"
That baffled wanderer, that lost one, I
Who for a whole month now have flown and flown,
And cannot land, and cannot find my own.

### 10

So drive back hating Love and loving Hate
To where, until we met, they had been thrown
Since infancy: forever lock that gate
And let them lacerate themselves alone,
Wild animals we never learned to tame,
But faced in growing anguish through the mist,
Elusive beasts we did not dare to name,
And whom we could not dominate or trust.

Now bury childish hunger, childish greed
In play-pen, zoo-pen, whatever pen will hold
The wild frustration and the starving need:
This is your method, so I have been told.
And mine? Stand fast, and face the animal
With the full force and pardon of the soul.

## 11

It does not mean that we shall find the place
Called peaceable in the old hopeful prints,
Where every tiger has a human face,
And every lamb can make a lion wince.
We met too late to know our meeting kind,
Too late for me to educate your heart,
Too late for you to educate my mind.
We shall be hurt again, and badly hurt;
There are torrents we cannot ever wall,
And there are arid deserts still to cross.
We shall not come where the green mercies fall,
To perfect grace, nor forget cruel loss—
But if we turn back now in such distress,
How find the way out of this wilderness?

## 12

Others have cherished, perhaps loved me more;
Through none have I endured so much disgrace,
And none has challenged me so deep and sore,
Brought to the surface such hard truth to face.
Our love has always been a two-edged sword
We handled brutally in self-protection:
The wounds we suffered were equal and were hard,
Yet your eyes looked in mine without deflection.
I never could imagine flight or fear,
I never doubted what the challenge was—
When angels and when furies fly so near,
They come to force Fate at a crucial pass.
They battle for some element or ghost:
What soul is being born to us, or lost?

## 13

Wild seas, wild seas, and the gulls veering close;
Dark islands float upon the silver Sound;
This weather is too somber for repose,
And I suffer the truth I have not found
As gulls suffer the wind and ride it too:
The speechless battle with the inner weather
That longs only to end with peace in you.
Oh, when you struck me, did you strike your mother?
Did I strike back to come into the dream?
(Nothing but storm and the wild seas today)
No wonder you withdrew and I still scream:
What present riches did we throw away,
To act the ancient drama out, until
The past and we cracked open and stood still?

## 14

For all the loving words and difficult
Work on the unregenerate heart, we foundered
Upon the seaming of a secret fault,
As rocks, mined by a flaw, are slowly sundered.
The need that joined us was too young and strong,
Yielding to violence and rage too soon,
Our every insight wrenched from some weak wrong.
This adult passion cried for a child's moon.
Not all the tenderness could set us free,
Nor all the steadfast hope through all the pain:
You never have been, you will never be
(The rock falls here, the secret flaw is plain)
My father, nor my son, nor any kin.
Where these words end, let solitude begin.

## 15

As I look out on the long swell of fields
Where winter wheat grows sparsely through the snow
And all lies fallow for those later yields,
Abandoned, quiet, where the pheasants go;
As skies move in slow motion overhead

To launch the wind and rain in a long gust,
Cold waves of air breaking on every homestead,
I beg my heart to lie still at long last.
But it thuds on, this animal gone blind,
And still enduring what strange marathon?
I must regard it with an acid mind:
Have done, poor beast, I say to it, have done,
And let pure thought rest on the winter sky
Without your stubborn question and reply.

### 16

The cat sleeps on my desk in the pale sun;
Long bands of light lie warm across the floor.
I have come back into my world of no one,
This house where the long silences restore
The esssence and to time its real dimension;
All I have lost or squandered I examine
Free of the wars and the long searing tension;
And I am nourished here after the famine.
Though this was time that we had planned to spend
Together, circled on the calendars,
To walk my woods for one weekend,
Last night I looked alone at the bright stars.
Nor time, nor absence breaks this world in two.
You hold me in your heart, as I hold you.

### 17

After a night of driving rain, the skies
Take on bright motion, radiant-obscure;
As thoughts like clouds traverse my human eyes,
Silence opens the world that I explore:
Mozartian gaiety, the lightest presence,
At last I welcome back my wandering soul
Into these regions of strange transcendence,
And find myself again, alive and whole;
Now intimations of a joy, so pure
It needs no human love to rest upon,
Come to me from the airs and reassure:
As I make the great leap to the unknown,

The flower of courage is given back to me,
Exact equivalent of agony.

## 18

These riches burst from every barren tree;
The brilliant mosses under balsam tell
All I have lost is given back to me,
And, naked as a newborn babe, I feel
The slightest change of air as an event,
Attend to every creak of the old floor
As to momentous words by angels sent,
Inner and outer worlds, mine to explore.
Take loneliness, take pain, and take it all!
Like some strong swimmer on the icy airs,
I glide and can survive the heart's own pitfall.
I tell you, I grow rich on these despairs:
For you I gladly yielded up my world,
Who now among enormous skies am hurled.

## 19

Where do I go? Nowhere. And who am I
Who sit alone in this small silent ark?
No one and no thing, but a breath or sigh,
Receptacle of light and flooding dark.
Now sunlight ripples through me in long waves,
Now the night rises, a tremendous tide,
And I am drowned or nearly. That what saves?
Who is the bridegroom of this ghostly bride?
A thinking heart, a feeling mind stripped bare
Of warmth and flesh, the soft delight and thong,
Reduced to a fine bone, as thin and spare,
I may now make an instrument for song:
Poetry, pour through me your ruthless word
As strong as once was love that used me hard.

## 20

Now silence, silence, silence, and within it
The leap of spirit upward and beyond;
We take the heart's world in our hands and spin it

Out to the distant stars above this ground,
And let it go at last, and let it go
With those illusions that we held too long;
Against our will now we are forced to grow
And push out from all safety into song.
This is one half of it, the saving grace;
The other, the dark struggle, as, like worms,
We riddle darkness, tunnel some small space
Where we can lie with patience through the storms.
And of these two, who knows where wisdom lies,
Deep in the earth, or wandering the skies?

## Moving In

I moved into my house one day
In a downpour of leaves and rain,
"I took possession," as they say,
With solitude for my domain.

At first it was an empty place
Where every room I came to meet
Watched me in silence like a face:
I heard the whisper of my feet.

So huge the absence walking there
Beside me on the yellow floor,
That one fly buzzing on the air
But made the stillness more and more.

What I possessed was all my own,
Yet not to be possessed at all,
And not a house or even hearthstone,
And never any sheltering wall.

There solitude became my task,
No shelter but a grave demand,
And I must answer, never ask,
Taking this bridegroom by the hand.

I moved into my life one day
In a downpour of leaves in flood,
I took possession, as they say,
And knew I was alone for good.

## Reflections by a Fire

*On moving into an old house in New Hampshire*

Fire is a good companion for the mind;
Here in this room, mellowed by sunlight, kind
After yesterday's thrall of rain and dark,
I watch the fire and feel some warm thoughts spark,
The seethe and bubble of some curious questions;
The air is full of small smiling suggestions.
For instance, why should window moldings lead
To ruminations upon love and need?
As if in their proportions, cleanly limned
By some plains craftsman, values had been framed
That tease us and have never been explained.

These windows frame a world, the rural scene
We lift our heads to scan, the village green,
Church spire, dirt road curving toward the hill:
Windows select the form and hold it still.
Almost their shape defines the shape of thought,
That spaciousness in a small region caught.
I wonder if the secret of dimension
Will come to me if I can pay attention,
And if I chose this house because I guessed—
And hoped that I would pass the crucial test—
That if the form was there I'd learn the rest.

Here now, rooted at last in my own home,
The small, intimate, dreamed-of kingdom come,
I ponder an old theme beside the fire—
How untraditional is the desire
That molds the great traditions of the mind!
For it is revolution that I find
Become the guest of old ideas at play,
(What strong belief structured the pillared doorway!)—
Reason and passion, freedom and tradition.
A changing style adapts a revolution,
And window moldings speak to man's condition.

Here private worlds rose to a grandeur given;
Men of this house left their dear hard won haven

And traveled many a lonely dusty mile
Because they represented an old style,
Because they stood by a form in the mind
(These doors and windows shape a man, and bind)
Knew what they meant and kept the meaning warm,
Taciturn, took a century by storm,
"Average, divine, original, concrete,"
Embodied freedom from a village street:
It is their ghosts I recognize and greet.

My windows frame a different world and season,
But here alive is passion and is reason.
The plain strong style supports my need to win
Some of its freedom and its discipline,
If not enlightenment, at least a tone
(Kind hopes that simmer in a house alone).
I dare myself, within this native shell,
To live close to the marrow, weather well,
Structure the bursts of love and poetry
So that both life and art may come to be
As strict and spacious as this house to me.

## Mud Season

In early spring, so much like a late autumn,
Gray stubble and the empty trees,
We must contend with an unwieldy earth.
In this rebirth that feels so much like dying,
When the bare patches bleed into raw mud,
In rain, in coarsening ooze, we have grown sluggard,
Cold to the marrow with spring's nonarrival:
To hold what we must hold is iron-hard,
And strength is needed for the mere survival.

By dogged labor we must learn to lift
Ourselves and bring a season in;
No one has ever called child-bearing easy,
And this spring-bearing also asks endurance.
We are strained hard within our own becoming,
Forced to learn ways how to renew, restore.
Though we were dazzled once by perfect snow,
What we have not has made us what we are.
Those surface consolations have to go.

In early spring, so much a fall of will,
We struggle through muds of unreason,
We dig deep into caring and contention;
The cold unwieldy earth resists the spade.
But we contend to bring a difficult birth
Out from the lack of talent, partial scope,
And every failure of imagination.
Science and art and love still be our hope!
What we are not drives us to consummation.

## Spring Planting

Conflict has been our climate for so long,
All we know gleaned from high jagged places,
And not a question there of right or wrong,
But only foothold on the mountain faces,
A balance for the self upon those sheer
Dizzying cliffs, then crampon, creep on somehow
To where we came to master at least fear;
In this way learned the little that we know:
And managed to exist, following hunches,
Acutely wary of the avalanches.

How then accept this ultimate plateau,
The calm arrival after the harsh climb?
For here we must learn simply how to grow,
Now we are safely balanced. There is time.
The self, gardener and not mountaineer,
Handles a spade or hoe, scatters new seed,
No wish for stronghold now there is no fear,
But to learn joy as well as rooted need.

A strange, a different, virtue is required
Here where the winds are kind, the temperate sun
Brings slowly up the green shoots we desired;
Now there is grace, and desperation gone.
Dear love, here we are planting—and so high,
Close to the cloud, visited by the snow—
A human world consoled by a great sky,
How grow from peace all that we wish to grow?
It is no small task. At last we have come
To plant our anguish and make for it a home.

## A Flower-Arranging Summer

The white walls of this airy house assume
Flowers as natural and needed friends;
All summer long while flowers are in bloom
Attentive expectation never ends.
The day begins with walking through wet grass
In a slow progress, to visit the whole garden,
And all is undecided as I pass,
For here I must be thief and also warden:
What must I leave? What can I bear to plunder?
What fragile freshness, what amazing throat
Has opened in the night, what single wonder
That will be sounded like a single note,
When these light wandering thoughts deploy
Before the grave deeds of decisive joy?

Later, I cut judiciously and fill my basket.
It's a fine clamor of unrelated voices,
As I begin the day's adventure and slow task,
The delicate, absorbing task of choices—
That lavender and pink that need some acid,
Perhaps a saffron zinnia, linen-crisp?
Or poppy's crinkle beside the rich and placid
Rose petal, and some erratic plume or wisp
To enhance cosmos, its flat symmetry,
And always the poised starry phlox in masses—
Sometimes I have undone the same bouquet
A dozen times in six different glasses,
A dozen times and still dissatisfied,
As if that day my wish had been denied.

Sometimes two poppies can compose a world,
Two and one seed-pagoda on a hairy stem,
Blood-red, vermilion, each entity unfurled
Clashes its cymbals in the silent room;
The scale so small, substance diaphanous,
Yet the reverberation of that twofold red
Has focused one room for me ever since,
As if an Absolute had once been said.
Sometimes the entire morning does get lost

In ochers, greenish-whites, in warm deep rose,
As I pick all the zinnias against frost,
Salmon, crude red, magenta—and who knows
What harsh loud chords of music sweep the room?
Both chords and discords, till the whole bright thing
Explodes into a brilliant cloud of bloom,
And the white walls themselves begin to sing.

And so the morning's gone. Was this to waste it
In a long foolish flowery meditation?
Time slides away, and how are we to taste it?
Within the floating world all is sensation.
And yet I see eternity's long wink
In these elusive games, and only there:
When I can so suspend myself to think,
I seem suspended in undying air.

## Hour of Proof

It is the light, of course, and its great ways;
It comes like a celestial charity
With warmth not coldness in its clarity,
And through the violent green its violet rays
Anatomize each single leaf to shine,
The flesh transparent to the nerves' design.

A blade of grass, a frond of goldenrod,
A branch of beech paled to translucent green,
This is a world where structure counts again,
Flooded through by the presence of the god.
These simple days are coursed by a great cry,
A storm of radiance sweeping from the sky.

And when it takes a crimson petal up,
The lifeblood shows so brilliant in the vein,
A single flower dominates the green,
As if all earth were lifted in this cup,
And life began to flow the other way,
Up from the brimming petal to the sky . . .

As if the echoing rocks were to reflect,
And every open meadow to fulfill
The place and time where dancing growth is still,
And light and structure gently intersect;
Not the cold but the warmth of *caritas*
Shows us the summer green for what it was.

The autumn light X-rays our sealed-up riches;
We find within the milkweed a strange milk,
The folded seeds in parachutes of silk
That will fly soon to fall on fields and ditches.
Passionate summer's hour of proof is come:
Go we, my love, and catch a falling sun!

## Der Abschied

Now frost has broken summer like a glass,
This house and I resume our conversations;
The floors whisper a message as I pass,
I wander up and down these empty rooms
That have become my intimate relations,
Brimmed with your presence where your absence blooms—
And did you come at last, come home, to tell
How all fulfillment tastes of a farewell?

Here is the room where you lay down full length
That whole first day, to read, and hardly stirred,
As if arrival had taken all your strength;
Here is the table where you bent to write
The morning through, and silence spoke its word;
And here beside the fire we talked, as night
Came slowly from the wood across the meadow
To frame half of our brilliant world in shadow.

The rich fulfillment came; we held it all;
Four years of struggle brought us to this season,
Then in one week our summer turned to fall;
The air chilled and we sensed the chill in us,
The passionate journey ending in sweet reason.
The autumn light was there, frost on the grass.
And did you come at last, come home, to tell
How all fulfillment tastes of a farewell?

Departure is the constant at this stage;
And all we know is that we cannot stop,
However much the childish heart may rage.
We are still outward-bound to obligations
And, radiant centers, life must drink us up,
Devour our strength in multiple relations.
Yet I still question in these empty rooms
Brimmed with your presence where your absence blooms,

What stays that can outlast these deprivations?
Now, peopled by the dead, and ourselves dying,

The house and I resume old conversations:
What stays? Perhaps some autumn tenderness,
A different strength that forbids youthful sighing.
Though frost has broken summer like a glass,
Know, as we hear the thudding apples fall,
Not ripeness but the suffering change is all.

# A Private Mythology
# (1961–1966)

*When I look back to my past days I find
myself envying the precarious position of high
officials, or sometimes thinking of becoming
a Buddhist monk. But after all I have come to
make my livelihood by resigning myself to
floating clouds and wind and flowers and birds.
In choosing this way of life, Li Po has
ruptured himself and old Tu Fu has grown
wretchedly thin, just like me, though I am
without any genius."*

Bashō

# The Beautiful Pauses

Angels, beautiful pauses in the whirlwind,
Be with us through the seasons of unease;
Within the clamorous traffic of the mind,
Through all these clouded and tumultuous days,
Remind us of your great unclouded ways.
It is the wink of time, crude repetition,
That whirls us round and blurs our anxious vision,
But centered in its beam, your own *nunc stans*
Still pivots and sets free the sacred dance.

And suddenly we are there: the light turns red,
The cars are stopped in Heaven, motors idle,
While all around green amplitude is spread—
Those grassy slopes of dream—and whirling will
Rests on a deeper pulse, and we are still.
Only a golf course, but the sudden change
From light to light opens a further range;
Surprised by angels, we are free for once
To move and rest within the sacred dance.

Or suddenly we are there: a hotel room,
The rumor of a city-hive below,
And the world falls away before this bloom,
This pause, high up, affecting us like snow.
Time's tick is gone; softly we come and go,
Barefoot on carpets, all joyfully suspended,
And there, before the open morning's ended,
The beautiful pause, the sudden lucky chance
Opens the way into the sacred dance.

I write this in October on a windless morning.
The leaves float down on air as clear as flame,
Their course a spiral, turning and returning;
They dance the slow pavane that gives its name
To a whole season, never quite the same.
Angels, who can surprise us with a lucky chance,
Be with us in this year; give us to dance
Time's tick away, and in our whirling flight
Poetry center the long fall through light.

## A Child's Japan

### 1

Before we could call
America home,
In the days of exile,
My image of holiness
Was Kobo Daïshi,
Young and beautiful,
Sitting on his lotus
In a thin gold circle
Of light.
He is with me still.

My father loved
Monasteries,
His fantasy, perhaps,
To abandon wife and child
And withdraw to a cell
Or an austere pavilion
With paper walls.

From my bed
Down the long dark hall
I could see him
Circled in light,
His back always bent
Over his desk,
Motionless for hours.

My mother
Treated flowers as individuals,
Hated clutter and confusion,
Invented marvelous games—
Paper skaters
Blown across a lacquer tray—
Knew how to make a small room
Open and quiet.

We lived in austere style
Through necessity

And because it suited us,
An artist, a scholar,
And their one child.
How Japanese the rain looked
In Cambridge,
Slanting down in autumn!
How Japanese, the heavy snow in lumps
On the black branches!

It is clear to me now
That we were all three
A little in love with Japan.

2

When I flew out into the huge night,
Bearing with me a freight of memory,
My parents were dead.

I was going toward
All they had left behind
In the houses where we had lived,
In the artful measure
And sweet austerity
Of their lives—
That extravagance of work
And flowers,
Of work and music,
Of work and faith.

I was flying home to Japan—
A distant relative,
Familiar, strange,
And full of magic.

# A Country House

*For Shio Sakanishi*

### 1

Sheltered under thick thatch,
The paper walls
Slide open
To bring those ancient members of the family,
Twelve plum trees,
Into the house,
Their gnarled black trunks
And their translucent flowers.
Two pots of pink cyclamen
And a parti-colored cat
Sun themselves
On the lintel.
I sit on a cushion
Facing a brilliant wall of books
And look out sideways,
Floated between
House and garden
In the spring air.

### 2

Rushing into the house
To get bird-glasses,
I forgot to take off my shoes—
Profanation
Of the clean, sweet-smelling
Grass mats.

Later,
Having worn socks
Into the garden,
I brought bits of dry grass
Onto the velvety blue rug
In the Western-style room.

Twice shamed!

# Kyoko

### 1

Her name is Kyoko,
Apricot,
Delicate, transparent
As the flower of the tree.

She tastes English
As if it were candied fruit—
"Mulberry," "nonchalant"—
And blushes at "avalanche";
Speaks of Virginia Woolf
As "specialist
In refined, pure,
And sensible mind."
Are there affinities?

Disaster
Shadows her cheek
Like the falling plum blossom.
When she smiles
Her ineffable smile
I know we have lost our way.

### 2

Kyoko says,
"Mat-cha will revive us."
We sit hopefully
In a forlorn tea house
Chilled by the March wind.

"First eat the rice cake;
Then lift the cup
In both hands
And turn it round
Two-and-a-half times.
Drink the hot tea
In exactly three sips
And a half,

Not forgetting
To wipe the cup's brim
Before you set it down."

So we drink mat-cha
And are restored
By ceremony—
And, perhaps, also
By the pale-green, foaming,
Legendary tea.

## Japanese Prints

*Four Views*
        *of Fujiyama*

        At Oiso,
        Floating above thatched roofs—
        Or was it a dream?

                        *

        At Hakone,
        Even rosy at dawn,
        A dead volcano.

                        *

        Above feathery bamboo,
        The harsh cone,
        Stark and white.

                        *

        In snowy amplitude
        Against a bright blue sky,
        The god himself.


                *On the Way to*
                        *to Lake Chuzen-ji*

                        We regretted the rain,
                        Until we saw the mists
                        Floating the mountains
                        On their dragon tails.


*Lake Chuzen-ji*

        Steel gray peaks,
        Dark blue lake,
        And an icy wind:
        The violence of Japan!

*Enkaku-ji,*
*Zen Monastery*

The fresh sweetness
Of Enkaku-ji—
Plum blossom
Or incense?

*Three Variations*
*on a Theme*

The lovely slanting rain
And, across the fields,
The hesitating flight
Of parasols.

*

Lines of slanting rain
And, across the fields,
Many small moons—
The paper umbrellas.

*

Moths? Or notes in music?
The parasols float
Above the fields
In the slanting rain.

*Seen from a Train*

How sad the thatch,
Abandoned, a mass of holes!
The peasant in each of us
Mourns the absence of smoke

*

In the distance
Heavy trucks roar past;
In the foreground,
An old man and his bullock
Take slow stately steps.

*

A sampler of fields,
Those leaning pagodas,
The haystacks,
A water wheel
And the white feet of the women,
Like rabbits.

*The Leopards*
        *at Nanzen-ji*

In the chill dark
Of an early spring morning,
The very soles of our feet
Are warmed
By the running of the leopards
On the golden screens!

            *

So swift, no paw touches ground—
And we are drawn back
To look at them once more,
As by the leaping of a flame.

*At Katsura,*
        *Imperial Villa*

In round straw hats,
Squatting in the rain
To weed the imperial moss—
Three mushrooms.

*The Inland Sea*

Islands as clouds,
Clouds as mountains,
A long dream that has no end—
And then the rain!

\*

Like ancient
Hard-to-decipher poems,
The islands write themselves
In mist.

*Tourist*

Boa constrictor
Who has swallowed
Too many temples!

*In a Bus*

An infant boy
Stares, solemn,
At my nose,
Then reaches out to touch it . . .
Elephant's trunk?

*Carp Garden*

The great carp,
Pale gold, vermilion,
Or black,
Move slowly
Like underwater kings—
Such elegance!

\*

Throw them a crumb—
The majestic ones
Become beggars
With ugly open mouths—
Such commotion!

## A Nobleman's House

### 1

After the palaces
Which simulate themselves
So well,
And each time they are rebuilt
Become a little less real,
A little more like lives
Frozen in an antique gesture
Which will never change,
What a relief
To come to an old house
Where the paper walls are torn,
Stained by a century of weather,
And even the stranger
Feels himself prolong
The sustained look of love
Toward the garden,
A little overgrown now
Despite the freshly raked sand.

### 2

The crooked old guide
Pauses a long time
Before he speaks,
As if he wished to be sure
That what he describes
Has been savored
Before he will give out
Information.

## Inn at Kyoto

Here the traveler
Becomes a child again,
Relearning every gesture,
Even how to eat,
Fastidious, with chopsticks,
A morsel at a time.
Meals delight the eye,
Resembling those
We invented for our dolls—
Honey in an acorn cup,
A daisy center
Laid on a maple leaf.
So two strawberries
Carefully nurtured
Against a sunny wall
May be presented
In a small flat basket
As the whole dessert.

(Kyoko and I
Fortify ourselves
For these aesthetic pleasures
By eating steak for lunch,
And so have the best
Of both worlds.)

When I stand up
I feel like an elephant,
Huge and out of place.
When I sit down again,
Illusion returns:
The padded kimono
Falls in great folds around me.

I inhabit a marvelous world
Where every sense is taught
New ways of perceiving.
What led me to dare this adventure?
To come alone—so far—

In middle age?
I light a cigarette
From the brazier at my side,
Watch the smoke curl,
And indulge in
Endless speculations.

We have learned to be silent,
Kyoko and I.

# An Exchange of Gifts

## 1

"When you come
Every evening,
Carrying heavy trays,
Kneeling to serve us,
You of the lovely middle-aged face
And sad eyes,
And never raise your lids,
Your dignity humbles.
Who are you?
What is your name?"

Kyoko translated for me.
But would the hermetic person
Accept the gift?

"My name is Eiko," she said,
And vanished,
Leaving us abashed,
Lacking a smile.

A week later,
After her day off,
She brought me a long box,
And in it a delicate fan.
Gravely we each bowed low,
Having exchanged presents,
And then at last,
Like the moon
From behind a cloud,
We saw her radiance.

## 2

Now it is coming to an end,
I see how I have lived,
Observing, recording
With a painter's impersonal eye:
Plum blossom,

White butterflies
Against a dark pine.
That feathery elegance, bamboo.
That fabulous mountain, a small rock.

So it has been for three weeks,
Until a single tired face,
The face of a servant,
Broke the pane of glass
Between me and all things:
I am inside the landscape.

For the Japanese
The nape of a neck
May evoke passion.
A tired face
Grounded my lightning.

The poems begin here

## The Stone Garden

*Ryoan-ji, fifteenth century*

When world is reduced
To clusters of rock

Strewn on bare sand,
World becomes essence.

> When tame sand is raked
> Into algebras

> Of orderly lines
> And orderly circles,

The wildness is framed—
Each rock is a magnet.

And each has been threaded
As if by haphazard

> And grouped into five
> Spaced constellations.

> The mind hovers here
> On the brink of creation.

Energy flows
From the magical scene,

So changeless and changing
It is never exhausted.

> In autumn a leaf falls
> And makes a notation.

> Sun shafting cloud
> Touches one rock alive.

Spring shadows delve
Pools here and there.

A snow-thatch in winter
Makes other distinctions.

> All things are suspended
> In shifting light and shades—

All but the theme itself:
Fifteen rocks and sand

Weaving a silent fugue
Down through the centuries,

So changeless and changing
It is never exhausted.

# Wood, Paper, Stone

*Katsura, former imperial villa*

## 1

Not for nothing, here,
Did architecture begin
As an enclosed space
Around a sacred tree.

Wooden pillars
Still create the rhythm
For a roof that rises
Strong as a wave
To that massive paean,
Its peak.

Below this shelter
Delicate walls
Consume light and shadow,
The house itself, a fugue
At play with weather and season—
Slide back a paper wall,
And trees, rocks, water
Come in as friends;
Slide back another,
And the moon is present,
That honored guest;
Close the paper translucence,
And a solitary heron
On a painted screen
Makes himself known
In the diffused light.

## 2

What aristocracy
Ever had such taste?
These austere palaces
Create a small cosmos
Where the minute

Becomes immense,
Not so much dwellings
For the body's comfort
As demanding ethos
For the soul.
Yet the mollusk
Which inhabited
These fabulous shells
Ended in the trivial
And died.
Even the poem,
Hedged in by the appropriate,
Ceased to breathe:
The haiku ends
In mannerism.

### 3

What we experience
Is hardly a way of life,
Exists in itself
Like geometry,
Is in fact a construction
Like Euclid's
And in the same way
Changes our mind.
We have to rethink
A way of being
That is chiefly
A way of looking.

### 4

So I watched a Japanese
Pause, spellbound,
Before seven steppingstones
As a Frenchman ponders
A line by Mallarmé;
I might have trod
On this casual pattern

Without being aware
That I trod on a marvel.

So I caught Kyoko's smile
Before the unexpected shape
Of a stone lantern;
I might have passed it by
Without catching
The artful humor.

So I listened
While a scholar expounded
The beauty of a cypress beam;
I might never have realized
That only barbarians
Disguise the genius of wood
With paint.

Neither a house,
Nor a garden,
Nor a rock, nor a tree
Would ever look the same again.

## The Approach—Calcutta

### 1

Landing
At four o'clock in the morning,
No man's hour,
I felt only dread.

Muslims drove a herd
Of gaunt cows
To the slaughter,
While the Hindus slept,
A shrouded multitude,
On the streets.
The whole city
Appeared to be
An improvised morgue.

Even a beggar's withered hand
Stretched out, inert,
As if already dead.

### 2

Here the gods themselves
Are too thick, too many,
Turn themselves into snakes,
Fish, or even boars,
And into sinuous lovers
Twined,
Erotic and restless,
In the coils of the eternal dance

Hot winds blew me
Hither and thither;
Barren,
Clouded by ignorance,
I peered out
At an impenetrable world:
People, animals,
Earth, gods,
Who none of them smiled.

## Notes from India

The letters ask:
You describe so much,
But how do you feel?
What is happening to you?
What I see is happening to me.


### 1. *At Bhubaneswar*

The ragged, rough, continental spaces
Where people never stop walking,
Alone or in long lines,
Over the dirt roads
Under hot, windy skies—
Dark figures walking
With the air of pilgrims
In saris faded
Purple, soft red, dark blue;
Clerks in white dhoties
Carrying black umbrellas,
Barefoot, erect;
Old men in dusty turbans
Naked to the waist;
Women carrying jugs on their heads;
Children in bright yellow and pink;
And, against the horizon,
Four carts and their bullocks
Walking, walking.
It has no beginning. It never ends.

Hunching themselves toward the sky,
Lifting the earth with them,
These temples seem to be waiting
For something that happened
Nine centuries ago.
Inside, the rough phallus stands erect;
Outside, the sculptured lovers embrace,
While black kites
Float on the sullen air,

And the world stands still,
An everlasting noon.

The fresh watercolor
Green of rice,
A flight of emerald parakeets,
The kingfisher's radiant blue—
Among the dead colors,
The cracked dry fields,
They meet the eye
As if earth burst
Like a pomegranate
To show its brilliance,
Fecundity of light.

The woman in a red sari,
Standing, thin presence
Among dessicated fields,
To watch us pass,
Looks as if she alone
Supported the whole sky.

In the temple pond
A young man prays
With folded hands,
His bronze chest bare
As he stands up to his waist
In the filthy, promiscuous,
Healing water.
Old women gossip under the banyan tree
While a Brahmin
Circumnavigates
The whitewashed temple
Chanting the morning prayer.
Little girls,
Damp hair stuck to their foreheads,
Dress in clean dresses—
The pool is troubled
Again and again
By the dark bodies

That go down through the scum
And return to the morning,
Smiling the smile of the newly washed.
In the distance a dove
Repeats itself.

I had been the woman
With a camera eye
Who notices everything
And is always watched,
The stranger on whom
No one smiled.
Then I slipped,
Fell headlong
In the red dust,
And at once the rickshaw boy
Is there at my side.
Thin expert hands
Feel hard for a break,
Then wipe the blood off
With a filthy cloth.
Worth a scraped knee
To land on this earth at last,
To be helped alive,
To be, in fact,
Touched!
The unsmiling people
Throng around me,
Smiling their pleasure.
Yes, I have landed.
Yes, I am alive.

### 2. *At Kanarak*

Out of the huge stone fortress,
Crouching within its four gates
And slowly sinking into the sand
With all its embracing figures,
Boring erotica,
Hourly more earthbound,
Caught on the wheel—

My field glasses
Suddenly caught
The smile of the Sun God—
A fleeting second,
But hours later
I was still
Under his spell.

### 3. *At Puri*

In the late afternoon sun
The Rajah's mildewed palaces,
Deep rose and ocher,
Sleep on the sands
Like couchant beasts,
Their eyes closed.
Where are the Rajahs now?

Three women:
We see their bare feet
Under the swinging door.
What are they up to
Behind the shutters
Of the hotel porch
In the burning afternoon?
At intervals
One lifts a hand with a duster,
Then lets it fall.
It takes much longer,
Apparently,
To do nothing
Than to do something
In air so heavy
It might be sand
Before the monsoon.

The Lord Jaganath
Brings to this sleepy city by the sea
The faces of all India.
Young ladies
In steel-rimmed glasses

Look studiously out
On this congregation:
Widows in white saris,
Those opulent balloons;
Mud-encrusted sadhus,
Sacred cows,
Fishermen and monkeys;
Black women with gold ornaments
In their nostrils;
Fine-featured Brahmins—
There is no end to the differences,
To the staggering variety
Among the pilgrims.

But when they go down to the sands
To be purified
They are a single pink and white wave
Going out together
To meet the multitudinous sea.

### 4. *At Fathpur Sikri*

Where once the Moghul princes
Rode with falcons on their wrists,
An old man
Sings a song
To make two monkeys dance.

## In Kashmir

Lovers of water and light
Rest on a silvery fleece,
Lost among willows and sheep.

The lake, a quiet eye,
Reflects on interchanges
Between clouds and the ranges.

And on this shallow mirror
The narrow long boats glide,
Turning white peaks aside.

While on his watching-pole,
A kingfisher, intent,
His long bill water-bent,

Makes a black, slanting line.
He focuses the scene,
The silver and the green.

Long pause, complete suspense—
And then the piercing dive
Shakes all the reeds alive.

The flash of sapphire blue
And mirror-breaking lance
Makes even mountains dance.

Back on his watching-pole
The king who got his wish
Swallows a little fish.

# The Sleeping God

*Vishnu-Narayana, Katmandu*

High in Nepal, the lock sprang at last:
There Vishnu lies entranced upon his pool,
And there I was touched deeply and held fast,

Was dreamed and delved, each nerve put to school,
Dreamed by this fertilizing power at rest
While anguish flowed away under his rule.

God, flower-fragile, open to the least,
Naked to every pulse of air and light,
More vulnerable in fact than any beast,

Young man relaxed in beauty, and so slight
He seems to float upon his dangerous sleep,
Daring to dream, exposed to the daylight.

He lies there on the coil, the massive loop
Of the eternal snake, a sovereign
Disarmed, without a wall, without a keep,

And renews all within his fertile reign,
And so, become the master of all space,
Is pure creation that can know no pain.

I saw him, naked, as a holy place,
A human Heaven which had learned to float
The universe upon a sleeping face.

And I, the Western one, was lost in thought,
Felt the lock spring, demons fly out,
And, all cracked open as the image caught,

Knew I was dreamed back to some ancient school
Where we are held within a single rule:
True power is given to the vulnerable.

## Birthday on the Acropolis

### 1

In the fifth grade
We became Greeks,
Made our own chitons,
Drank homemade mead,
And carved a small Parthenon
Out of Ivory soap.
It never seemed real,
The substance too soft,
An awkward miniature.
But over these labors
Athene towered,
Life-size.
She was real enough.

She was mine, this one,
From the beginning,
Not she of the olive,
But she of the owl-eyes,
A spear in her hand.

Any day now the air would open,
Any day . . .

### 2

Forty years later
I was hurled to the bright rock,
Still merged with the dark,
Edgeless and melting,
The Indian ethos—
Stepped out from the plane
To stand in the Greek light
In the knife-clean air.

Too sudden, too brilliant.
Who can bear this shining?
The pitiless clarity?
Each bone felt the shock.

I was broken in two
By sheer definition:

Rock, light, air.

3

I came from the past,
From the ancient kingdoms
To this youth of my own world,
To this primary place.

I stood at the great gate
On my fiftieth birthday,
Had rounded the globe
Toward this Acropolis,
Had come round the world
Toward this one day:

O Pallas Athene,
You of the shining shield,
Give me to stand clear,
Solid as this, your rock,
Knowing no tremor.

Today, you, Pandrosos,
Who cherish the olive,
Bring from my battered trunk
The small silver leaves,
Fresh and unshielded.

Make the olives rich
In essential oil;
May the fruit fall lightly
As small drops of rain
On the parched fields.
Protect the small trees.

Today, you, Aglauros,
Pure prow of Athens,
Poise me in balance
So that all clarity
May meet all mystery
As on the spear's point.

### 4

When proportion triumphs,
When measure is conscious,
Who is to protect us from arrogance?

The presence of the gods. They are here:
Fate's ambiguities and jealous Athene.

No, it is not a place for youth,
This bastion where man's reason grew strong.
These pillars speak of mature power.

Imagined as white, they are rough gold,
The spaces between them open as justice
To frame mountains
And the distant, blue, world-opening sea.

### 5

On my fiftieth birthday I met the archaic smile.
It was the right year
To confront
The smile beyond suffering,
As intricate and suffused
As a wave's curve
Just before it breaks.

Evanescence held still;
Change stated in eternal terms.
Aloof. Absolute:
The criterion is before us.

On my fiftieth birthday
I suffered from the archaic smile.

## Nostalgia for India

In the clean, anodyne
Hotel room in Athens,
I am suddenly homesick for
The Indian night
And my dark cell
In Orissa
Where I was visited
By a white lizard
With emerald eyes,
By an articulate frog,
And sometimes, very late,
By a wandering shrew.
The lizard chittered
And danced;
The shrew ran compulsively
Along the wall;
The frog,
When I lifted him up,
Gave a single heart-rending cry
In my unmysterious
White room,
I miss the chittering,
The cry of despair,
The silent, lunatic trot—
It is too sane here for words.

## On Patmos

An early morning island;
Underfoot, rockrose,
Crushed thyme, no grass.
Gold seams of wheat
Strewn across rocky pasture,
Through the chill, bright air
Imagination bounds
Like a goat.

Here John,
Resting his head
In a scooped hollow
Of his cave,
Knew poverty
And pure elation,
Here, "in the isle that is called Patmos,"
Felt the prophetic wind,
In the place of exile.

## Another Island

And this too was Greece:
Water so clear
A jellyfish looked opaque;
Silence so transparent
A voice could scratch it
Like a pane of glass;
A long crescent of white sand
Where we found
Not a broken hand of Aphrodite
Nor a silver coin,
But small pink shells,
The rockrose
White as foam
Under the dark pines—
And across the translucent sea
Another island
Floating on a dark blue line.

## At Lindos

"What are ruins to us,
The broken stones?"
They made for the sea,
These elementals
Possessed by Poseidon.
"And what is Athene?"
The sun flamed around them.
The waters were clear green.

What compelled us
To face the harsh rock?
Why did we choose
The arduous stairways?
There lay the crescent
Of white sand below us,
And the lucky swimmers.

But at last we came out,
Stood high in the white light,
And we knew you, Athene,
Goddess of light and air,
In your roofless temple,
In your white and gold.
We were pierced with knowledge.
Lucidity burned us.
What was Poseidon now,
Or the lazy swimmers?
We looked on a flat sea
As blue as lapis.
We stood among pillars
In a soaring elation.

We ran down in triumph,
Down the jagged stairways
To brag to the bathers,
But they rose up to meet us
Mysterious strangers
With salt on their eyelids,
All stupid and shining.

So it is at Lindos,
A place of many gods.

# At Delphi

The site echoes
Its own huge silences

Wherever one stands,
Whatever one sees—

Narrow terror of the pass
Or its amazing throat,
Pouring an avalanche of olives
Into the blue bay.

Crags so fierce
They nearly swallow
A city of broken pillars,
Or Athene's temple,
Exquisite circle,
Gentled on all sides
By silvery leaves.

Eagles floating
On high streamers of wind,
Or that raw cleft,
Deep in the rock,
Matrix
Where the oracle
Uttered her two-edged words.

Wherever one stands,
Every path leads to Fate itself:
"Speak! Speak!"

But there is no answer.

Choose the river of olives.
Choose the eagles.
Or choose to balance
All these forces,
The violent, the gentle;
Summon them like winds
Against a lifted finger.
Choose to be human.

Everyone stands here
And listens. Listens.
Everyone stands here alone.

I tell you the gods are still alive
And they are not consoling.

I have not spoken of this
For three years,
But my ears still boom.

## Ballads of the Traveler

### 1

*O traveler, tell, what marvels did you see*
*In old Japan over the shining sea?*
In Kyoto I saw a garden planned
As a closed figure of rocks arranged in sand;
Raked lines by natural shapes inhabited
Are seen as mountains and an ocean-bed—
The severe limits release as well as rule.
Here the imagination goes to school:
I saw a thinking garden, rocks and sand,
Become a dream that I must understand.

*O tell us, friend, what wonders there are*
*In far Kashmir, in ancient Srinagar?*
In Srinagar, a world of snow and sky
Where the *shikaras*, shallow long boats, ply,
I saw a kingfisher, watching a fish,
Sit his long pole with concentrated wish—
Wait, wait, wait—then take the dive
And swallow his bright wriggling catch alive.
In Kashmir the sheer sapphire of that flight
Hit like a shot the bull's-eye of delight.

*In Katmandu?* The sacred black bull dozes.
The painted eye of Buddha never closes.
There Vishnu rests. I saw the great god sleeping
With all life in his vulnerable keeping.
He floats, stone hands clasped under his head,
Wholly exposed there on his watery bed.
And I was moved to see a god defined
As vulnerable, as open floating mind,
His power expressed in simply being there,
Open to every trick of earth and air.

*O traveler, you have told us many things:*
*How to relate them, as the ballad sings?*
An abstract garden, a wild kingfisher,
And a stone god lying in naked splendor—
Each had a daring spontaneity

Within strict limits, so each spoke to me.
My eyes beheld them; now they see me, hold
Me in their presence and begin to mold
And work their changes in the slow blood stream.
They are the dreamers. I become the dream.

2

*About the holy places, traveler, tell us.*
*What of Benares? Nara? What of Patmos?*
In Nara, ancient sleeping city, deer
May safely graze; pagodas, tier on tier,
Float on the mist, their sumptuous Te Deum.
There are too many Buddhas in the dark museum.
The image blurs, but I shall always see,
But I still keep, the moment of Chugu-ji,
The shining peace, the absolute consent
Of pure compassion's image in the convent,
Kwannon so subtly molded, every line
Is drawn to marry human and divine.
Nor man, nor woman, nor intellect, nor sense,
The godhead smiles and prayer is simply Presence.

After this pure, cool image of Japan,
I feared Benares and God-drunken man.
No one had told me how it would be,
And I was not prepared for majesty.
Above pale blue, the palaces stand high,
A circle of great walls against the sky.
Below them, endless flights of stairs go down;
Below them, endless multitudes of men—
In emerald and white, in pink and brown—
Go down into the river at the dawn.
When the sun rises, man worships and is free.
All unprepared for such tranquillity,
I saw the hungry multitudes made one
There in the Ganges at the rising sun.

Much later Patmos, a stark, barren island,
An empty place where only exiles land.
Thyme and wild roses, here and there a sheep;

Rock, barren rock, this island like a keep.
No multitude here, but each soul alone;
Great height; wind whistling in the bone.
Here John carved himself out a little bed
Within his cave, a hollow for his head.
Disturbing angels shouted without cease;
He wrote The Revelation to have peace.
On Patmos, soul is soul alone and wild,
And once became half-lion and half-child.
I walked the rocks. I knew the angels were
Not gentle in that wilderness, but fire.

## Lazarus

*Anglo-Saxon*, A.D. *1000*
*Chichester Cathedral*

### 1

From the rock and from the deep
The sculptor lifts him out aware.
This is the dead man's waking stare.
This is a man carved out of sleep.
The grave is hard; the walls are steep.

The sculptor lifts him out aware
From the rock and from the deep.
We watch with awe; we watch and keep
The heavy world he has to bear.
The sculptor lifts him out, aware.
Huge forlorn eyes open from sleep.
When morning comes, what do we keep?

The heavy world he has to bear.
He comes from the unconscious deep
With what to give and what to keep?
Lazarus lifts huge hands in prayer.
He turns the world round in his stare.

He sees his late death everywhere.
It hurts his eyes, he has to care.

Now broken from the rock of sleep,
He comes toward us from the deep

To face once more the morning star,
To see us desperate as we are.

And Lazarus relearns despair.
His look is grave; his gaze is deep

Upon us, men carved out of sleep
Who wish to pray but have no prayer.

### 2

A weightless traveler, I too come back
From miles of air, from distant and strange lands,

Put on my house again, my work, my lack,
And looking down at my own clumsy hands,
Feel courage crack.

How can I answer all these needs at once?
Letters and friends and work and flowers?
They sweep me back in their devouring glance
To carry off my calm and hoarded powers
In a huge pounce.

That heavy thickness as of new-mown hay
Flung down in heaps over a tentative fire—
How lift my smothered flame up to the day?
Have I come back depleted of desire,
To tire and fray?

At last I hear the silence in the room:
The buried self is breaking through to be,
And Lazarus is calling me by name.
At last I slowly lift the poem free,
One-pointed flame.

I hear, "to live as one already dead"—
A voice heard in Japan long months ago.
The sweat of *muga* starts on my forehead.
It is the sweat poets and dancers know,
In joy and dread.

Images flow together in that heat,
And confused numbers thread a single line.
Detached from all except the living beat,
I dance my way into complex design
On weightless feet.

## "Heureux Qui, Comme Ulysse . . ."

### *After Du Bellay*

Happy the man who can long roaming reap,
Like old Ulysses when he shaped his course
Homeward at last toward the native source,
Seasoned and stretched to plant his dreaming deep.
When shall I see the chimney smoke once more
Of my own village; in a fervent hour
When maples blaze or lilac is in flower,
Push open wide again my plain white door?

Here is a little province, poor and kind—
Warmer than marble is the weathered wood;
Dearer than holy Ganges, the wild brook;
And sweeter than all Greece to this one mind
A ragged pasture, open green, white steeple,
And these whom I have come to call my people.

## Of Havens

Though we dream of an airy intimacy,
Open and free, yet sheltering as a nest
For passing bird, or mouse, or ardent bee,
Of love where life in all its forms can rest
As wind breathes in the leaves of a tree;
Though we dream of never having a wall against
All that must flow and pass, and cannot be caught,
An ever-welcoming self that is not fenced,
Yet we are tethered still to another thought:
The unsheltered cannot shelter, the exposed
Exposes others; the wide open door
Means nothing if it cannot be closed.

Those who create real havens are not free,
Hold fast, maintain, are rooted, dig deep wells;
Whatever haven human love may be,
There is no freedom without sheltering walls.
And when we imagine wings that come and go
What we see is a house, and a wide-open window.

## The House in Winter

The house in winter creaks like a ship.
Snow-locked to the sills and harbored snug
In soft white meadows, it is not asleep.
When icicles pend on the low roof's lip,
The shifting weight of a slow-motion tug
May slide off sometimes in a crashing slip.
At zero I have heard a nail pop out
From clapboard like a pistol shot.

All day this ship is sailing out on light:
At dawn we wake to rose and amber meadows,
At noon plunge on across the waves of white,
And, later, when the world becomes too bright,
Tack in among the lengthening blue shadows
To anchor in black-silver pools of night.
Although we do not really come and go,
It feels a long way up and down from zero.

At night I am aware of life aboard.
The scampering presences are often kind,
Leaving under a cushion a seed-hoard,
But I can never open any cupboard
Without a question: what shall I find?
A hard nut in my boot? An apple cored?
The house around me has become an ark
As we go creaking on from dark to dark.

There is a wilder solitude in winter
When every sense is pricked alive and keen
For what may pop or tumble down or splinter.
The light itself, as active as a painter,
Swashes bright flowing banners down
The flat white walls. I stand here like a hunter
On the *qui vive*, though all appears quite calm,
And feel the silence gather like a storm.

## Still Life in Snowstorm

Outside, an April snow,
Beautiful but unwelcome,
Encloses all we know
In a wild whitening gloom
Thick light without a shadow
That makes the world a room.

Inside, the hearth aflame,
Red roses, and a warm
Chardin, all frame
Some charm within the storm
That turns the enclosed room
Open to worlds of balm.

"Still life with eggs and fish";
Outside the snow falls fast.
Inside we have our wish,
Redeemed from every past.
Light on a flat brown dish
Holds life so still at last,

Holds life so rich and full,
Beyond all change or chance,
No drop of it can spill.
From this pure eminence
We watch the wild snow fall,
And we are safe for once.

## A Fugue of Wings

Each branching maple stands in a numb trance,
A skeleton fine-drawn on solid air,
No sound or motion . . . summer's rippling dance
Has been abstracted to this frozen stare
Of black, and blue, and white.

Until the wings—the wings alive!—excite
The marbled snows; and perpendiculars
Of tree and shadow thrown across the light
Are shivered by minute particulars.
The opening phrase is there.

A fugue of wings darts down through the still air,
A dancing passage of staccato notes,
Now up, now down, and glancing everywhere,
Glissandos of black caps and neat white throats.
Here come the chickadees!

Parabolas fly through the static trees;
They dart their pattern in like an assault
On all defined and frozen boundaries.
Their beat is off-beat. Chickadees exalt
Erratic line, rebound,

Hang upside down, play with the thread of sound,
But cede to those blue bandits, the big jays,
Who plummet down like daggers to the ground;
The rhythm changes with their boisterous ways;
They scream as they feed.

Now finches flock down to the scattered seed,
Disperse on the forsythia's light cage
In rosy clusters, sumptuous indeed—
With them, we come into a gentler passage.
They form a quiet cloud

Thick on the ground, and there in concert crowd.
A nuthatch follows, he of modest mien
And dangerous beak; the music grows too loud.
The fugue is cluttered up. What we have seen,
What we did hear is done.

Until woodpeckers take it up, and drum
The theme; finches fly up with jays;
A whirling passage spirals the fugue home.
Afterward silence, silence thronged with praise
Echoes and rounds the phrase.

## An Observation

True gardeners cannot bear a glove
Between the sure touch and the tender root,
Must let their hands grow knotted as they move
With a rough sensitivity about
Under the earth, between the rock and shoot,
Never to bruise or wound the hidden fruit.
And so I watched my mother's hands grow scarred,
She who could heal the wounded plant or friend
With the same vulnerable yet rigorous love;
I minded once to see her beauty gnarled,
But now her truth is given me to live,
As I learn for myself we must be hard
To move among the tender with an open hand,
And to stay sensitive up to the end
Pay with some toughness for a gentle world.

## Learning about Water

### 1

That summer
We learned about water—
The long suspense,
Dry winds, and empty sky.
The village parched
Slowly,
Till leaves began to shrivel
On the tallest trees.

The Indians would dance.
We had no rite. No refuge.
To wait, endure, listen
To the weathervane creak
Through the tense, hot night,
And, waking to a new sickness,
Turn the word *rain*
In our mouths
Like a cool pebble,
As one well after another
Went dry

### 2

The time came for me.
My rich well,
Fed by three springs
Of clear cool water,
Deeper than I could touch
The bottom of
With a long pole—
The never-failing well
Was milked out.

The pump rattled on
Like a broken record
Repeating one word,
*Water*,
*Water*.

But when I shut it off,
I heard the silence,
The dry silence of
No water,
No water,
No water.

### 3

One morning
The great leaves of the squash
Had fallen, wrinkled,
Round the raw brown stems.
I hid from the curse
Like a goddess
Who has lost her power
To keep life alive.
"This," said the Egyptians
In the time of drought,
"Is the taste of death."

## An Artesian Well

The well drillers
Came in winter.
Their dinosaur,
Rigid and slimy,
Towered over the house;
For days it loomed there
Smothered in snow.

At last they roused it.
The steel phallus
Began its pounding
Through the thick clay,
Through layers of sand,
Searching out rock—
Tons of violence
Against tons of inertia.
Could any good
Come of this battle?

Stopped by a boulder,
They exploded their way down,
Brutal, with dynamite—
Sprayed the house with mud.
What had happened below?
What frightful splinters?
What shudder?
What shattering?
Could any good come of this
Rape of the earth?

It went on all day—
No escape, no haven—
Through what resistance,
Toward what anguish?
I who paced the floors
Had commanded it.

And locked together
In gritty patience,
We pressed cold faces

Against the cellar wall,
Listening, listening
For the hard rock.
And at last
The stone resounded:
We had reached the ledges.

In that troubled year
I had not seen luck's face
But at last I did.
Eighty-five feet down
Under our hands,
Under the clay,
Under the sand,
Under the boulders,
Under the long drought
In the hard ledges,
We struck it—
Five gallons a minute.
Flowing water
Sprang out in a fountain.

I wept like a woman
Who, after long labor,
Sees the living child.
I felt like the earth.

# A Late Mowing

Neighbors have come to mow my ragged field,
And three old horses bring the autumn home.
Now the blond waving grasses must come down,
And all the tasseled splendor has to yield.

Good-by to summer's feasts and variations:
Two months ago there burst into great praises,
White as enamel, in rich constellations,
A sky of stars flung down to earth as daisies.

When they went out, the fireflies were showing;
The green field pulsed with intermittent fire,
And the cats crept a jungle of desire
After these softest stars within the mowing.

Good-by to ringing of the sumptuous changes—
To black-eyed Susan, paintbrushes and plantain,
Clear buttercups and cloudy asters, mullein.
Good-by and praise to the high-summer ranges.

Now all those stars are altered in their courses,
And the rich field cut back to rock and root;
My neighbors with their three autumnal horses
Cut down the ghosts of summer with the fruit.

Winter, be gentle to this earth you keep,
To buried root and all that creeps and flies,
While overhead your dazzling daisy skies
Flower in the cold, bright mowing that will keep.

## A Country Incident

Absorbed in planting bulbs, that work of hope,
I was surprised by a loud human voice,
"Do go on working while we talk. Don't stop!"
And I was caught upon the difficult choice—
To yield the last half-hour of precious light,
Or to stay on my knees, absurd and rude.
I willed her to be gone with all my might,
This kindly neighbor who destroyed a mood.
I could not think of next spring any more;
I had to reassess the way I live.
Long after I went in and closed the door
I pondered on the crude imperative.

What it is to be caught up in each day
Like a child fighting imaginary wars,
Converting work into this passionate play,
A rounded whole made up of different chores
Which one might call haphazard meditation.
And yet an unexpected call destroys
Or puts to rout my primitive elation.
Why be so serious about mere joys?
Is this where some outmoded madness lies,
Poet as recluse? No, what comes to me
Is how my father looked out of his eyes,
And how he fought for his own passionate play.

He could tear up unread and throw away
Communications from officialdom,
And, courteous in every other way,
Would not brook anything that kept him from
Those lively dialogues with man's whole past
That were his intimate and fruitful pleasure.
Impetuous, impatient to the last,
"Be adamant, keep clear, strike for your treasure!"
I hear the youthful ardor in his voice
(And so I can forgive a self in labor).
I feel his unrepentant, smiling choice
(And so must ask indulgence of my neighbor).

## Second Thoughts on the Abstract Gardens of Japan

Having sent memory to prowl,
I look at treasure it has brought.
These artful images, this tight control,
Trouble my thought.

Clearly, we can but sense some peril
In a stone waterfall?
Made of hard rocks, and absolutely sterile,
The urgent spill

Is fossilized and frozen still,
A static death in changing air:
Motion deprived of motion always will
Suggest despair.

This is volcanic country. Violence lives
Close under cultivated surfaces.
There is a smell of brimstone. What of chaos?

Country of myth—an emperor
Once exiled all deciduous trees:
No falling leaf was to remind his splendor
That landscapes freeze.

Beneath his will and his bravado
Death was at work; the untamed beast
Lay there in wait; and every fall of snow
Could mar the feast.

Those provinces with bound-up feet—
The dwarf tree in a cramping pot—
Might just explode one day, force a root out,
Or die of rot.

A vital image kills an empire. And between
Rigidity and chaos, the garden looks sick.
Life is organic. Life is somewhere else.

Having sent memory to scan
The famous garden, it came back
Troubled from a too-formalized Japan
To take a look

At quaint New England wilderness.
Rocky, and twisted by harsh wind,
Nearer to Hell than Heaven though it is,
It rests the mind.

The rock that looms out of my field,
Controlled by neither man nor God,
Brings with it aster, a rich yield,
And goldenrod.

It is closer to nature than to chaos,
My woods cut just enough to show the mountain,
And that's not much, but gives a kind of order.

Still, the big question rests on form,
On form and what form must imply:
I am not one of those who worship storm,
Or the wild sky—

Unbuttoned ego. I have staked
My life on controlled native powers;
My garden, so untamed, still has not lacked
Its hard-won flowers.

Like abstract gardens bound to will,
Some poems which began in flaming,
Died later of excessive, detached skill
And overtaming.

What is appeased is chaos in such cases.
Its opposite, rigidity, takes over.
I want good violence to find organic form.

## A Village Tale

Why did the woman want to kill one dog?
Perhaps he was too lively, made her nervous,
A vivid terrier, restless, always barking,
And so unlike the gentle German shepherd.
She did not know herself what demon seized her,
How in the livid afternoon she was possessed,
What strength she found to tie a heavy stone
Around his neck and drown him in the horse-trough,
Murder her dog. God knows what drove her to it,
What strength she found to dig a shallow grave
And bury him—her own dog!—in the garden.

And all this while the gentle shepherd watched,
Said nothing, anxious nose laid on his paws,
Tail wagging dismal questions, watched her go
Into the livid afternoon outside to tire
The demon in her blood with wine and gossip.
The gate clanged shut, and the good shepherd ran,
Ran like a hunter to the quarry, hackles raised,
Sniffed the loose earth on the haphazard grave,
Pressing his eager nose into the dust,
Sensed tremor there and (frantic now) dug fast,
Dug in, dug in, all shivering and whining,
Unearthed his buried friend, licked the dry nose
Until a saving sneeze raised up the dead.

Well, she had to come back sometime to face
Whatever lay there waiting, worse than horror:
Two wagging tails, four bright eyes shifting—
Moment of truth, and there was no escape.
She could face murder. Could she face redeeming?

Was she relieved? Could she perhaps pretend
It had not really happened after all?
All that the village sees is that the dog
Sits apart now, untouchable and sacred,
Lazarus among dogs, whose loving eyes
Follow her back and forth until she dies.

She gives him tidbits. She can always try
To make them both forget the murderous truth.

But he knows and she knows that they are bound
Together in guilt and mercy, world without end.

## The Horse-Pulling

All was dingy and dull in late afternoon.
We sat on wooden benches, silent and sweating,
Becalmed there beyond expectation,
Sated by blue-ribbon sheep and candy, waiting
On the dusty last day of the fair to see
The horse-pulling (whatever that might be).

So underplayed a scene in the exhausted air,
We almost fell asleep. Why had we come,
I mean on earth at all, not only here?
Loud-speakers blared out some lost child's name.
The horses sneezed and shuffled in the heat.
We were all waiting with lead in our feet.

And then the darkness lifted like a dream.
We were back in some old heroic place—
Three men led in the first competing team.
Horses? No, gods! An arrogance of grace,
A dancing lightness held in three dwarfs' hands,
They swept like music past the silent stands.

It was brute power contained in sweet decorum,
The noble heads held high as in a frieze.
Relaxed and gay, they made the dust a forum.
It took us like a shout, tears in our eyes,
As they pranced up so lightly to the test,
And turned and were caught at the throat and chest.

They took the lunge as if their fire could grate
The awkward stone-boat forward like a feather,
Staggered under the impact of dead weight,
Like shackled furies almost knelt together,
Huge haunches quivering under the jolt—
And spent their lightning in a single bolt.

The small men who had cursed and lashed out—
Dwarfs bending gods to their little will—
Gentled them to a walk and led them out,
Set free again—but oh, they trembled still!—
While judges measured the courage of their bound
In hard-won inches on the battleground.

We watched this act repeated there for hours,
As some teams failed, and all grew more tense,
Stone piled on stone to strain utmost powers;
At last the weight was cruel and immense,
Our favorites winning to the last assay,
Cheered as they danced in, still relaxed and gay.

Win or lose now, we stood on our bench
To cheer this final test, as the brute force
Burst against dead weight in a violent wrench
Of nerve and muscle. The attack was fierce,
But spent too soon. They buckled to their knees,
And lost the day, heads bent upon the frieze.

The failure seemed some inward-fated doom:
How could they win, or we, who had given
Our hearts to horses all that afternoon?
We left, unnerved, and came shadowed home,
Thinking of all who strive and lose their grip,
And of wild hopes, and of the tragic slip.

# Franz, a Goose

It is contagious as a dance,
The morning exultation of the goose
Whose inappropriate name is Franz.
Daily he comes, majestic and snow white,
To put his private pond to use,
To stand alone within the rite
And make ovations to pure self-delight.

As one long waving sleeve, he dips
Soft neck, blue eyes, and orange beak
Deep into waters where the magic sleeps,
Now up, now down, in hieratic bliss,
Gives them the dark caress they seek,
Then lifts that giant arm, weapon and grace,
To shake a rain of diamonds to the grass.

Can one describe superb-as-these ablutions,
This royal pomp as a mere daily wash?
The liquid phrase, the lovely repetitions?
His squawks are murmurs now. He sings.
Then with one huge triumphant splash
Enters the pond and beats his wings:
"I am the goose of geese, the king of kings!"

Who could resist such pride or pull it down?
Yet who resist one tentative caress,
To touch the silken neck that wears a crown?
I dare the irresistible in play,
To meet a cold blue eye and blazing hiss;
His person rises up in terrible dismay,
And talks of the indignity all day.

Followed at just two paces by his queen
(Possessive murmurs lead her gently on),
He makes his progress like a paladin,
Explains, complains of the awesome caress,
And how pomp trembled yet achieved disdain,
Assures her that he gave a fatal hiss,
Assures himself what a great goose he is.

## Lovers at the Zoo

They come, expectant, as to a minor Heaven,
Those dear, enchanted, and lost human pairs,
The city lovers with no natural haven,
Except to watch the lemurs in their lairs
Or contemplate the furriness of bears,
As if this place of cages and despairs
Were reminiscent of a childhood day,
Falsely preserved by memory as gay.

They wander, smiling vaguely, and attend
The eternal seal in his round pool, who weaves
A sumptuous pattern where the ripples blend
In massive undulations, humps and heaves,
Then rumples up the surface as he leaves
For joys unseen below, whom nothing grieves.
He's gone, and they go too; they hardly talk,
And seem suspended slightly as they walk.

The raccoons are affectionate and rude;
The porcupine, face to the wall, is cross;
The baby elephants play with their food
A game of blow-your-oats or catch-and-toss.
"Do turtles hibernate?" "They look like moss."
"And have you ever seen an albatross?"
Lost in the Rousseau world, they wander through
This dream where all the animals come true.

Men trembled long ago and found no word
Before the Sphinx's hard, incurious gaze
(And no one tells us whether sphinxes purred),
But here where wilderness is tamed and plays,
And here where questions sleep through the long days,
Imagination leaps and lovers blaze,
For here the sensual world is so beguiling
They go out hand in hand, shamelessly smiling.

## Death and the Turtle

I watched the turtle dwindle day by day,
Get more remote, lie limp upon my hand;
When offered food he turned his head away;
The emerald shell grew soft. Quite near the end
Those withdrawn paws stretched out to grasp
His long head in a poignant dying gesture.
It was so strangely like a human clasp,
My heart cracked for the brother creature.

I buried him, wrapped in a lettuce leaf,
The vivid eye sunk inward, a dull stone.
So this was it, the universal grief:
Each bears his own end knit up in the bone.
Where are the dead? we ask, as we hurtle
Toward the dark, part of this strange creation,
One with each limpet, leaf, and smallest turtle—
Cry out for life, cry out in desperation!

Who will remember you when I have gone,
My darling ones, or who remember me?
Only in our wild hearts the dead live on.
Yet these frail engines bound to mystery
Break the harsh turn of all creation's wheel,
For we remember China, Greece, and Rome,
Our mothers and our fathers, and we steal
From death itself rich store, and bring it home.

# Elegy for Meta

*For Meta Budry Turian*

Fiery, the tender child
From the beginning burned,
And that beginning hard.
She raced like a young colt,
Spirit no man could tame,
And yet so warm and wild
All nature toward her turned,
Came to her hand and word—
Extravagance, revolt:
    The signature was flame.

Consumed and self-consuming,
Life sparkled in her hand
And shot out stars of fire
That vanished in the air,
Then showered once again.
A sparkler ever-blooming,
How could she understand
Her never-spent desire?
They called her Douce-Amère:
    The signature was pain.

Such spirits always shed,
Remake, and once more lose
Their strange and starry brightness
In phosphorescent glory:
Not blest themselves, must bless.
So she nursed, sheltered, fed
The starved, the wounded, always
With an angelic lightness;
Yet in her tragic story,
    The signature was loss.

We loved, we come to hallow
The great famished heart,
The flame (at last at rest)
That never hurt nor harmed.
She only ran to give,

And only burned to show
Where abnegations start.
How difficult at best
A life so wild and charmed!
The signature was love.

## Death of a Psychiatrist

### *For Volta Hall*

#### 1

Now the long lucid listening is done,
Where shame and anguish were subtly opposed:
His patients mourn this father as their own.

Each was accepted whole and wholly known,
Down to the deepest naked need exposed.
Now the long lucid listening is done.

For the raw babe, he was a healing zone.
The cry was heard; the rage was not refused.
Each has a father to mourn as his own.

When someone sees at last, the shame is gone;
When someone hears, anguish may be composed,
And the long lucid listening is done.

The ghostly child goes forth once more alone,
And scars remain, but the deep wound is closed.
Each has a father to mourn as his own.

A guiltless loss, this shines like a sun,
And love remains, but the deep wound is closed.
Each has a father to mourn as his own,
Now the long lucid listening is done.

#### 2

It was not listening alone, but hearing,
For he remembered every crucial word
And gave one back oneself because he heard.

Who listens so, does more than listen well.
He goes down with his patient into Hell.

It was not listening alone, but healing.
We knew a total, yet detached response,
Harsh laugh, sane and ironical at once.

Who listens so, does more than merely pity,
Restores the soul to its lost dignity.

It was not listening alone, but sharing,
And I remember how he bowed his head
Before a poem. "Read it again," he said.

Then, in the richest silence he could give,
I saw the poem born, knew it would live.

It was not listening alone, but being.
We saw a face so deeply lined and taut
It wore the passion of dispassionate thought.

Because he cared, he heard; because he heard,
He lifted, shared, and healed without a word.

## Conversation in Black and White

*For Saunders Redding*

At first we sat imprisoned in this place
Where snow was falling; curtains fell to screen us,
And neither of us had a human face.
The falling snow lay silently between us.

We had no features; like two floating moons,
One black, one white, we had to strain and peer
Across a shifting, thick, ambiguous gloom,
Wanting to tear it open and see clear.

But who would summon a single word so warming
It might green over the snow-battened ground,
Or make clear daylight shine through all the harming—
And who would dare to touch the tribal wound?

Bring me your bitterness, and I will give
My guilt. Until these two have been exchanged,
Symbolic tokens between alien princes,
Still the snow falls, and still we are estranged.

But who could risk the heart out of the skin?
Then anything seemed possible but lies.
It was: cry out or stay locked up within
The moonlike faces without human eyes.

We had to risk more than we could afford,
More than men summon easily so soon,
As if I were your secret self, my lord,
And you my secret friend, no stranger moon.

And then our human anguish did look through;
The wounded at the wounded, open, stared.
The morning of the world was not more blue
Than the one world-embracing look we shared.

## The Walled Garden at Clondalkin

### 1

For a long time they merely left it there;
They were too full of pity and distress
To breathe again that choked and choking air.
The rusty gate closed on a wilderness.
The walled garden, an old dying princess
From a lost country, had grown very strange.

A snow of petals fell on the rich loam:
*Gloire des Mousseux*, Star of Holland, Night,
Ladies in waiting in a spacious room,
Those roses dressed in small clouds of light.
All, all, destroyed, invaded, overgrown,
The formal beauty gone, formal delight,
And none to reclaim now, to heal, save
Order and beauty buried here alive.

"Where are the roses gone?" they whispered, shaken,
On those rare sad occasions when they stood,
Remembering the safer land of childhood,
And saw this feverish ruin, overtaken
By squitch and groundsel and the woody nightshade.
"Where are the goldfish, where the pond?" And fled,
As children do, this world grown out of range.
"The times have changed. We cannot help the change."

### 2

Think of her, remember
The brilliant queen of phlox,
Of roses without number,
Disciplined in box—
Of delphinium, the duchess;
A hierarchy of herbs
Sweetened in order—
Rosemary, mignonette—
Each trim border.
She wore mock orange

In her green hair,
Marvelously strange;
The birds in the air,
The goldfish came
To her summer voice
And knew her by name.
Her peaches were choice.
Camellias, carnations
In warm glass prisons
Were subject nations.
Her winter princes
Were hothouse quinces.
Walled, glassed in vain
The royal domain:
Quick grows the grass
In flowery places,
And the wilderness,
And the crude green faces.

3

And there it was they found him, standing splendid
Among his thirty thousand leeks and lettuces,
The empty pots filled and the glass all mended;
He looked indulgently on the sweet peas,
Lord of the greenhouses, and so pure his joy
That as he picked a peach, he seemed a boy.

The garden was scarcely breathing when he came,
A gentle foreigner with mud on his shoes,
Not even a relative, poor, and of no fame,
A water-carrier, trundler of wheelbarrows.
Quiet and slow, his pockets full of seeds,
He cleared the wild disordered past of weeds.

"All gone, all sold, the princess dead, my dears!"
The peacock on the wall screamed and was still.
The watchers felt perplexed by shifting years.
They suffered all the past and future till
The tangled skein was smoothed out and resolved,
As if some hopeless muddle had been solved.

No new world ever could have moved them as
This dying one revived by gentleness.
Their thoughts were tender for the dying princess,
But not for her sake did the warm tears rise:
They gave this homage to patient human ways,
The hired man's common and heroic days.

## A Recognition

*For Perley Cole*

I wouldn't know how rare they come these days,
But I know Perley's rare. I know enough
To stop fooling around with words, and praise
This man who swings a scythe in subtle ways,
And brings green order, carved out of the rough.
I wouldn't know how rare, but I discover
They used to tell an awkward learning boy,
"Keep the heel down, son, careful of the swing!"
I guess at perils and peril makes me sing.
So let the world go, but hold fast to joy,
And praise the craftsman till Hell freezes over!

I watched him that first morning when the dew
Still slightly bent tall, toughened grasses,
Sat up in bed to watch him coming through
Holding the scythe so lightly and so true
In slow sweeps and in lovely passes,
The swing far out, far out—but not too far,
The pause to wipe and whet the shining blade.
I felt affinities: farmer and poet
Share a good deal, although they may not know it.
It looked as easy as when the world was made,
And God could pull a bird out or a star.

For there was Perley in his own sweet way
Pulling some order out of ragged land,
Cutting the tough, chaotic growth away,
So peace could saunter down a summer day,
For here comes Cole with genius in his hand!
I saw in him a likeness to that flame,
Brancusi, in his Paris studio,
Who pruned down, lifted from chaotic night
Those naked, shining images of flight—
The old man's gentle malice and bravado,
Boasting hard times: "It was my game!"

"*C'était mon jeu!*"—to wrest joy out of pain,
The endless skillful struggle to uncloud

The clouded vision, to reduce and prune,
And bring back from the furnace, fired again,
A world of magic, joy alone allowed.
Now Perley says, "God damn it!"—and much worse.
Hearing him, I get back some reverence.
Could you, they ask, call such a man your friend?
Yes (damn it!), and yes world without end!
Brancusi's game and his make the same sense,
And not unlike a prayer is Perley's curse.

So let the rest go, and heel down, my boy,
And praise the artist till Hell freezes over,
For he is rare, he with his scythe (no toy),
He with his perils, with his skill and joy,
Who comes to prune, to make clear, to uncover,
The old man, full of wisdom, in his prime.
There in the field, watching him as he passes,
I recognize that violent, gentle blood,
Impatient patience. I would, if I could,
Call him my kin, there scything down the grasses,
Call him my good luck in a dirty time.

## Joy in Provence

*For Camille Mayran*

I found her, rich loser of all,
Whom two wars have stripped to the bone,
High up on her terrace wall
Over vineyards asleep in the sun—
Her riches, that ample scene
Composed in the barn's round door;
Her riches, rough cliff and pine,
Aromatic air—and no more.
Here, seasoned and sweetened by loss,
She thrives like thyme in the grass.

This woman's feet are so light,
So light the weight of her eyes
When she walks her battlements late
To harvest her thoughts as they rise,
She is never caught, only wise.
She rests on the round earth's turning
And follows the radiant skies,
Then reads Pascal in the morning.
And, walking beside her, I learned
How those dazzling silences burned.

On the longest day of June,
When summer wanes as it flowers
And dusk folds itself into dawn,
We had shared the light drenched hours.
We lay on rough rock in the sun,
Conversing till words were rare,
Conversing till words were done,
High up in the pungent air,
Then silently paced while the moon
Rose to dance her slow pavane.

The wine from a meditation
Was mine to drink deeply that night,
O vintage severe, and elation,
To be pressed out of loss, and from light!
Alive to her thought, yet alone,

As I lay in my bed, close to prayer,
A whisper came and was gone:
"Rejoice" was the word in the air.
But when the silence was broken,
Not by me, not by her, who had spoken?

## Baroque Image

*For Any Artist*

He angled the bright shield
To catch the setting sun,
And dazzled the whole field,
Enemy, friend, as one.

Who had the nerve to borrow
That sheen in a dark hour,
The arrows of Apollo
And the god's blinding power?

They did not sense the wound
Behind that tilted shield—
For he could hardly stand
Who dazzled the whole field!

# As Does New Hampshire
# (1967)

# Winter Night

An hour ago that birch, that pine
Were separated intervals,
A light-and-shadow world of line
Against the washed-in mountain walls.
But who can say the darkness *falls*?
It floods in a whole new design.

What was distinct now subtly changes;
The focus opens to include
Some scarcely noted interchanges
Between the mountains and the wood,
As, rising slowly where they stood,
The long dark comes to take the ranges.

There is no telling how starlight
Falls across shining fields of snow,
And brings this darker kind of bright
That flows back through the afterglow
And floods the earth with vivid blue,
A different radiance called Night.

## March-Mad

The strangely radiant skies have come
To lift us out of winter's gloom,
A paler more transparent blue,
A softer gold light on fresh snow.
It is a naked time that bares
Our slightly worn-down hopes and cares,
And sets us listening for frogs,
And sends us to seed catalogues
To bury our starved eyes and noses
In an extravagance of roses,
And order madly at this season
When we have had enough of reason.

## Metamorphosis

Always it happens when we are not there—
The tree leaps up alive into the air,
Small open parasols of Chinese green
Wave on each twig. But who has ever seen
The latch sprung, the bud as it burst?
Spring always manages to get there first.

Lovers of wind, who will have been aware
Of a faint stirring in the empty air,
Look up one day through a dissolving screen
To find no star, but this multiplied green,
Shadow on shadow, singing sweet and clear.
Listen, lovers of wind, the leaves are here!

## Apple Tree in May

"But it's falling already,
Falling!" I cried,
"So fast and so soon . . ."
The flowering bride
Of the white May moon.

My neighbor and I
Stood there by the door,
Petals floating down
For a moment more
On the green and the brown.

Then the boy at my side
Whom I hardly know
Said, "The petals leave"
(As he turned to go)
"But you mustn't grieve.

For they fall, you know,
To make the fruit
For the harvest moon:
Don't you be put out
So fast, so soon."

It was falling already,
Falling, my joy,
So fast and so soon,
When a country boy
Said, "The harvest moon . . ."

## A Glass of Water

Here is a glass of water from my well.
It tastes of rock and root and earth and rain;
It is the best I have, my only spell,
And it is cold, and better than champagne.
Perhaps someone will pass this house one day
To drink, and be restored, and go his way,
Someone in dark confusion as I was
When I drank down cold water in a glass,
Drank a transparent health to keep me sane,
After the bitter mood had gone again.

## Stone Walls

They make me wince, such vivid dreams rise up
When I walk second growth and witness spill
Tumbled by roots, with no one there to keep
Stones balanced or to care whether the wall
Stays firm or not. But truth is, after all,
They were not built for walls so much as dumps
For the waste stuff the glacier left behind.
Farmers have fought this land of rocky bumps
For two long centuries, always to find
Daily frustration of a cussèd kind
Where clever men gave up for lack of hope.
Some heroes piled the walls, saw thick-wooled sheep
Cropping at last on the rough grassy slope.
It looked like hard-won riches that would keep—
Until Australia came in on the cheap,
To ruin all that they had labored for
Those cruel years before the Civil War.

I wince, and then I feel a kind of pride.
Those who left, left to find the easy plain.
Those who stayed learned to grow some rock inside,
To build hard substance out of loss and pain,
Start thinking fresh, endure and contain.
Those who stayed either grew ingenious
Or degenerate—the pivot, mind.
Stark need fostered inventive genius.
Mills, factories of every kind
Sprang from that losing fight against the land.

Although I came here from a different waste—
The fertile fields war crossed and recrossed
(England and Belgium married in my past)—
I feel like memory itself these pastures lost,
And wince at what the broken stone walls cost.

## A Guest

My woods belong to woodcock and to deer;
For them, it is an accident I'm here.

If, for the plump raccoon, I represent
An ash can that was surely heaven-sent,

The bright-eyed mask, the clever little paws
Obey not mine, but someone else's laws.

The young buck takes me in with a long glance
That says that I, not he, am here by chance.

And they all go their ways, as I must do,
Up through the green and down again to snow,

No one of us responsible or near,
But each himself and in the singular.

When we do meet, I am the one to stare
As if an angel had me by the hair,

As I am flooded by some ancient bliss
Before all I possess and can't possess.

So when a stranger knocks hard at the door,
He cannot know what I am startled for—

To see before me an unfurry face,
A creature like myself in this wild place.

Our wilderness gets wilder every day
And we intend to keep the tamed at bay.

# A Grain of Mustard Seed
# (1967–1971)

# A Ballad of the Sixties

In the West of the country where I was
Hoping for some good news,
Only the cripple had fire,
Only the cripple knew the mind's desire;
In the wheel chair alone
Poetry met the eyes
That see and recognize,
There in the wizened bone.
    For only the ill are well,
    And only the mad are sane.
    This is the sad truth plain,
    The story I have to tell.

In the North of the country where I saw
The anxious rich and the angry poor,
Only the blasted life had reason;
Only the stricken in the bitter season
Looked out of loss and learned
The waste of all that burned,
Once cared and burned.
    For only the mad are sane,
    And only the lost are well,
    And loss of fire the bane
    Of this season in Hell.

In the South of the country where I passed
Looking for faith and hope at last,
Only the black man knew
The false dream from the true;
Only the dark and grieving
Could be the still believing.
    For only the ill are well,
    Only the hunted, free,
    So the story I have to tell
    In the South was told to me.

In the East of the country where I came
Back to my house, back to my name,
Only the crazy girl was clear

That all has been betrayed to fear;
Only the mad girl knew the cost,
And she, shut up from wind and rain
And safely plucked out from her pain,
Knew that our love is lost, is lost.

For only the sick are well;
The mad alone have truth to tell
In the mad games they play—
Our love has withered away.

## The Rock in the Snowball

*For Mark Howe*

How little I knew you, Mark, to mourn so wild
As if death hit square in the mouth today.
That snowball held a rock and it hurt hard.
But even outraged, am I still a child
To take death with raw grief and howl my way
Hand against mouth to ward off the word?

How little I knew you, Mark, but for the blue
Those deep-set eyes shafted across a room
To prick the ghost of pride or of pretense,
That straight look into doom if it were true,
That poker look that made our laughter bloom
And burned up sham like paper with a glance.

You were exposed, a man stripped down to care,
Thin as a boy, tempest-torn as a boy,
And sick with pity, conscious-caught-and-bound.
Courage is easy—every boy can dare—
But harder to keep justice from that joy,
And bury feeling, your self-inflicted wound.

And yet you burned. And yet you burned so deep,
Mastering fire, controlling fire with wit,
That eulogies seem pale beside your breath,
And we are fools, since you would not, to weep.
We mourn ourselves, that is the truth of it,
Hit by the savage rock that is your death.

Whatever end we hoped with you alive,
To be those few, and happy, growing old,
To talk of battles shared, of false and true,
That light is gone. We shall have to survive
As remnants in a world turned grim and cold
Where once we laughed at Hell itself with you.

# The Invocation to Kali

*... The Black Goddess Kali, the terrible one of many names, "dif-*
*ficult of approach," whose stomach is a void and so can never be*
*filled, and whose womb is giving birth forever to all things ...*
                                                    Joseph Campbell

### 1

There are times when
I think only of killing
The voracious animal
Who is my perpetual shame,

The violent one
Whose raging demands
Break down peace and shelter
Like a peacock's scream.

There are times when
I think only of how to do away
With this brute power
That cannot be tamed.

I am the cage where poetry
Paces and roars. The beast
Is the god. How murder the god?
How live with the terrible god?

### 2

*The Kingdom of Kali*

Anguish is always there, lurking at night,
Wakes us like a scourge, the creeping sweat
As rage is remembered, self-inflicted blight.
What is it in us we have not mastered yet?

What Hell have we made of the subtle weaving
Of nerve with brain, that all centers tear?
We live in a dark complex of rage and grieving.
The machine grates, grates, whatever we are.

The kingdom of Kali is within us deep.
The built-in destroyer, the savage goddess,
Wakes in the dark and takes away our sleep.
She moves through the blood to poison gentleness.

She keeps us from being what we long to be;
Tenderness withers under her iron laws.
We may hold her like a lunatic, but it is she
Held down, who bloodies with her claws.

How then to set her free or come to terms
With the volcano itself, the fierce power
Erupting injuries, shrieking alarms?
Kali among her skulls must have her hour.

It is time for the invocation, to atone
For what we fear most and have not dared to face:
Kali, the destroyer, cannot be overthrown;
We must stay, open-eyed, in the terrible place.

Every creation is born out of the dark.
Every birth is bloody. Something gets torn.
Kali is there to do her sovereign work
Or else the living child will be stillborn.

She cannot be cast out (she is here for good)
Nor battled to the end. Who wins that war?
She cannot be forgotten, jailed, or killed.
Heaven must still be balanced against her.

Out of destruction she comes to wrest
The juice from the cactus, its harsh spine,
And until she, the destroyer, has been blest,
There will be no child, no flower, and no wine.

### 3

#### *The Concentration Camps*

Have we managed to fade them out like God?
Simply eclipse the unpurged images?
Eclipse the children with a mountain of shoes?
Let the bones fester like animal bones,

False teeth, bits of hair, spilled liquid eyes,
Disgusting, not to be looked at, like a blight?

Ages ago we closed our hearts to blight.
Who believes now? Who cries, "merciful God"?
We gassed God in the ovens, great piteous eyes,
Burned God in a trash heap of images,
Refused to make a compact with dead bones,
And threw away the children with their shoes—

Millions of sandals, sneakers, small worn shoes—
Thrust them aside as a disgusting blight.
Not ours, this death, to take into our bones,
Not ours a dying mutilated God.
We freed our minds from gruesome images,
Pretended we had closed their open eyes

That never could be closed, dark puzzled eyes,
The ghosts of children who went without shoes
Naked toward the ovens' bestial images,
Strangling for breath, clawing the blight,
Piled up like pigs beyond the help of God. . . .
With food in our stomachs, flesh on our bones,

We turned away from the stench of bones,
Slept with the living, drank in sexy eyes,
Hurried for shelter from a murdered God.
New factories turned out millions of shoes.
We hardly noticed the faint smell of blight,
Stuffed with new cars, ice cream, rich images.

But no grass grew on the raw images.
Corruption mushroomed from decaying bones.
Joy disappeared. The creature of the blight
Rose in the cities, dark smothered eyes.
Our children danced with rage in their shoes,
Grew up to question who had murdered God,

While we evaded their too attentive eyes,
Walked the pavane of death in our new shoes,
Sweated with anguish and remembered God.

## 4

### *The Time of Burning*

For a long time, we shall have only to listen,
Not argue or defend, but listen to each other.
Let curses fall without intercession,
Let those fires burn we have tried to smother.

What we have pushed aside and tried to bury
Lives with a staggering thrust we cannot parry.

We have to reckon with Kali for better or worse,
The angry tongue that lashes us with flame
As long-held hope turns bitter and men curse,
"Burn, baby, burn" in the goddess' name.

We are asked to bear it, to take in the whole,
The long indifferent beating down of soul.

It is the time of burning, hate exposed.
We shall have to live with only Kali near.
She comes in her fury, early or late, disposed
To tantrums we have earned and must endure.

We have to listen to the harsh undertow
To reach the place where Kali can bestow.

But she must have her dreadful empire first
Until the prisons of the mind are broken free
And every suffering center at its worst
Can be appealed to her dark mystery.

She comes to purge the altars in her way,
And at her altar we shall have to pray.

It is a place of skulls, a deathly place
Where we confront our violence and feel,
Before that broken and self-ravaged face,
The murderers we are, brought here to kneel.

## 5

It is time for the invocation:

Kali, be with us.
Violence, destruction, receive our homage.
Help us to bring darkness into the light,
To lift out the pain, the anger,
Where it can be seen for what it is—
The balance-wheel for our vulnerable, aching love.
Put the wild hunger where it belongs,
Within the act of creation,
Crude power that forges a balance
Between hate and love.

Help us to be the always hopeful
Gardeners of the spirit
Who know that without darkness
Nothing comes to birth
As without light
Nothing flowers.

Bear the roots in mind,
You, the dark one, Kali,
Awesome power.

## After the Tiger

We have been struck by a lightning force
And roaring like beasts we have been caught
Exulting, bloody, glad to destroy and curse.
The tiger, violence, takes the human throat,

Glad of the blood, glad of the lust
In this jungle of action without will,
Where we can tear down what we hate at last.
That tiger strength—oh it is beautiful!

There is no effort. It is all success.
It feels like a glorious creation.
An absolute, it knows no more or less,
Cannot be worked at, is nothing but sensation.

That is its awful power, so like release
The animal within us roars its joy.
What other god could give us this wild peace
As we run out, tumultuous to destroy?

But when the tiger goes, we are alone,
Sleeping the madness off until some dawn
When human eyes wake, huge and forlorn,
To meet the human face that has been torn.

Who was a tiger once is weak and small,
And terribly unfit for all he has to do.
Lifting a single stone up from the rubble
Takes all his strength. And he hurts too.

Who is a friend here, who an enemy?
Each face he meets is the same savaged face
Recovering itself and marked by mystery.
There is no power left in this sad place—

Only the light of dawn and its cold shadow.
How place a cool hand on some burning head?
Even compassion is still dazed and raw.
The simplest gesture grates a way toward need.

After the violence peace does not rise
Like a forgiving sun to wash all clean,

Nor does it rush out like some fresh surmise
Without a thought for what the wars have been.

"I too am torn" or "Where is your hurt?"
The answer may be only silences.
The ghostly tiger lives on in the heart.
Wounds sometimes do not heal for centuries.

So the peace maker must dig wells and build
Small shelters stone by stone, often afraid;
Must live with a long patience not to yield.
Only destruction wields a lightning blade.

After the tiger we become frail and human
The dust of ruins acrid in the throat.
Oh brothers, take it as an absolution
That we must work so slowly toward hope!

## "We'll to the Woods No More, the Laurels Are Cut Down"

*At Kent State*

The war games are over,
The laurels all cut down.
We'll to the woods no more
With live ammunition
To murder our own children
Because they hated war.

The war games are over.
How many times in pain
We were given a choice—
"Sick of the violence"
(Oh passionate human voice!)—
But buried it again.

The war games are over.
Virile, each stood alone—
John, Robert, Martin Luther.
Still we invoke the gun,
Still make a choice for murder,
Bury the dead again.

The war games are over,
And all the laurel's gone.
Dead warrior, dead lover,
Was the war lost or won?
What say you, blasted head?
*No answer from the dead.*

# Night Watch

## 1

Sweet night nursing a neighbor—
The old lady lifts her hands
And writes a message
On the air—
Gently I lay them down.
Sudden motion
Might shift the bandage
Over one eye.

Across the hall
A woman moans twice.
I alone am not in pain,
Wide-awake under a circle of light.

Two days ago in Kentucky
I was the sick child,
Sick for this patchy, barren earth,
For tart talk,
Dissatisfaction,
Sharp bitter laughter,
Sick for a granite pillow.

Among that grass soft as silk,
Those courtesies, those evasions,
I was sick as a trout
In a stagnant pond.

Wide-awake,
I weigh one thing against another.
The old lady will see
Better than before;
The woman who moaned
Sleeps herself whole again.

Sweet, innocent night
In the hospital
Where wounds can be healed!

2

The birds sing
Before dawn,
And before dawn
I begin to see a little.
I hold the old warm hand in mine
To keep it from clawing
The bandage,
And to comfort me.

I am happy as a mother
Whose good baby sleeps.

In Kentucky
They are spurned mothers,
Curse the children
And their hot black eyes,
Hard from not weeping;
Remember the old days,
Dear pickaninnies,
Mouths pink as watermelon.

What happens
When the baby screams,
Batters the barred cage of its bed,
Wears patience thin?

What happens
When the baby is six feet tall,
Throws stones,
Breaks windows?

What happens
When the grown man
Beats out against us
His own hard core,
Wants to hurt?

In the white night
At the hospital
I listened hard.
I weighed one thing

Against another.
I heard, "Love, love."
(Love them to death?)

And at dawn I heard a voice,
"If you love them,
Let them grow."

### 3

The convalescent
Is quick to weak rage
Or tears;
In a state of growth
We are in pain,
Violent, hard to live with.
Our wounds ache.
We curse rather than bless.

### 4

"I hate them," she said.
"They spoil everything," said
The woman from Baltimore.
"It is not the dear old town
I used to know."

I felt pain like an assault,
The old pain again
When the world thrusts itself inside,
When we have to take in the outside,
When we have to decide
To be crazy-human with hope
Or just plain crazy
With fear.

(The drunken black in the subway
Will rape you, white woman,
Because you had bad dreams.)

Stomach pain, or vomit it.
In Kentucky I threw up
One whole night.
Get rid of this great sick baby

We carry around
Or go through the birth-sweat again.
Lazy heart,
Slow self-indulgent beat,
Take the sick world in.

### 5

In Baltimore
The black who drove me to the airport
Seemed an enormous, touchable
Blessing.
"When you give a speech," he told me,
"And you get that scared feeling,
Take a deep breath. It helps."

Comfort flowed out from him.
He talked about pain
In terms of healing.
Of Baltimore, that great hospital
Where the wounds fester
Among azaleas and dogwood,
The lovely quiet gardens,
"We are making things happen,"
Said the black man.
"It is going to be beautiful."
He had no doubt.

Wide awake in the hospital
In the morning light,
I weighed one thing against the other.
I took a deep breath.

## Proteus

They were intense people, given to migraine,
Outbursts of arrogance, self-pity, or wild joy,
Affected by the weather like a weather vane,
Hungry for glory, exhausted by each day,
Humble at night and filled with self-distrust.
Time burned their heels. They ran because they must—

Sparkled, spilled over in the stress of living.
Oh, they were fickle, fluid, sometimes cruel,
Who still imagined they were always giving;
And the mind burned experience like fuel,
So they were sovereign losers, clumsy winners,
And read the saints, and knew themselves as sinners.

Wild blood subdued, it was pure form they blest.
Their sunlit landscapes were painted across pain.
They dreamed of peaceful gardens and of rest—
And now their joys, their joys alone remain.
Transparent, smiling, like calm gods to us,
Their names are Mozart, Rilke—Proteus.

# A Last Word

*For my students at Wellesley College*

Whatever we found in that room was not easy,
But harder and harder, and for me as well,
Fumbling for words when what we fumbled for
Could not be spoken, the crude source itself;
The clever people had no news to tell.

The best failed. That is the way it is.
The best knew what we were mining after
Was not to be reached or counted in an hour.
The worst poems, maybe, became fertile,
And we knew moments of pure crazy laughter.

Often you came into that room becalmed,
Your faces buttoned against the afternoon.
If the hour occasionally opened into trees,
If we digressed, leaving the subject flat,
Well, we were fighting hard against the gloom.

The vivid battle brought us within the hour
Out of the doldrums together, edged and warm.
At any instant the fall of a mask
Released some naked wisdom; an open face
Surprised itself and took our world by storm.

For you, I trust, the time was never wasted;
For me, driven to dig deep under my cover,
Into the unsafe places where poets operate,
There is no grief; too much was taken and given,
More than administrators can discover.

And so you go your ways, and I go mine,
Yours into the world at last, and mine away—
To some adventure on another planet.
Whatever failed or you still hoped to do
Will grow to harvest in some other way,

Not against the stream of a college, but
Toward an ordering of the spirit in pure air
Where no one is bound by custom, or so engined

Toward immediate goals, and trapped by time:
Your poems will happen when no one is there.

And when the angel comes, you will remember
Our fierce encounter, beyond devious ways,
Not at the end of some blank corridor—
Outside all walls, the daring spirit's wrench
To open up a simple world of praise!

## Girl with 'Cello

There had been no such music here until
A girl came in from falling dark and snow
To bring into this house her glowing 'cello
As if some silent, magic animal.

She sat, head bent, her long hair all aspill
Over the breathing wood, and drew the bow
There had been no such music here until
A girl came in from falling dark and snow.

And she drew out that sound so like a wail,
A rich dark suffering joy, as if to show
All that a wrist holds and that fingers know
When they caress a magic animal.
There had been no such music here until
A girl came in from falling dark and snow.

## The Muse as Medusa

I saw you once, Medusa; we were alone.
I looked you straight in the cold eye, cold.
I was not punished, was not turned to stone—
How to believe the legends I am told?

I came as naked as any little fish,
Prepared to be hooked, gutted, caught;
But I saw you, Medusa, made my wish,
And when I left you I was clothed in thought . . .

Being allowed, perhaps, to swim my way
Through the great deep and on the rising tide,
Flashing wild streams, as free and rich as they,
Though you had power marshaled on your side.

The fish escaped to many a magic reef;
The fish explored many a dangerous sea—
The fish, Medusa, did not come to grief,
But swims still in a fluid mystery.

Forget the image: your silence is my ocean,
And even now it teems with life. You chose
To abdicate by total lack of motion,
But did it work, for nothing really froze?

It is all fluid still, that world of feeling
Where thoughts, those fishes, silent, feed and rove;
And, fluid, it is also full of healing,
For love is healing, even rootless love.

I turn your face around! It is my face.
That frozen rage is what I must explore—
Oh secret, self-enclosed, and ravaged place!
This is the gift I thank Medusa for.

## For Rosalind

### *On Her Seventy-fifth Birthday*

Tonight we come to praise
Her splendor, not her years,
Pure form and what it burns—
Who teaches this or learns?—
Intrinsic, beyond tears,
Splendor that has no age.
Take your new-fangled beauties off the stage!

The high poise of the throat
That dazzled every heart—
Who was not young and awed
By beauty so unflawed
It seemed not life, but art?—
Terrible as a swan
Young children, deeply moved, might look upon.

The blazing sapphire eyes—
They looked out from a queen.
Yet there was wildness near;
She glimmered like a deer
No hunter could bring down.
So warm, so wild, so proud
She moved among us like a light-brimmed cloud.

The way her dresses flowed!
So once in Greece, so once . . .
Passion and its control.
She drew many a soul
To join her in the dance.
Give homage fierce as rage.
Take your new-fangled beauties off the stage!

## The Great Transparencies

Lately I have been thinking much of those,
The open ones, the great transparencies,
Through whom life—is it wind or water?—flows
Unstinted, who have learned the sovereign ease.
They are not young; they are not ever young.

Youth is too vulnerable to bear the tide,
And let it rise, and never hold it back,
Then let it ebb, not suffering from pride,
Nor thinking it must ebb from private lack.
The elders yield because they are so strong—

Seized by the great wind like a ripening field,
All rippled over in a sensuous sweep,
Wave after wave, lifted and glad to yield,
But whether wind or water, never keep
The tide from flowing or hold it back for long.

Lately I have been thinking much of these,
The unafraid although still vulnerable,
Through whom life flows, the great transparencies,
The old and open, brave and beautiful . . .
They are not young; they are not ever young.

## Friendship: The Storms

How much you have endured of storm
Among sweet summer flowers!
The black hail falls so hard to do us harm
In my dark hours.

Though friendship is not quick to burn,
It is explosive stuff;
The edge of our awareness is so keen
A word is enough.

Clouds rise up from the blue
And darken the sky,
And we are tossed about from false to true
Not knowing why.

After this violence is over
I turn my life, my art,
Round and around to discover
The fault in my heart—

What breeds this cruel weather,
Why tensions grow;
And when we have achieved so much together,
What breaks the flow.

God help us, friendship is aware
That where we fail we learn;
Tossed on a temperament, I meet you there
At every turn.

In this kaleidoscope
Of work and complex living,
For years you buttressed and enlivened hope,
Laid balm on grieving.

After the angry cloud has broken
I know what you are—
How love renews itself, spoken, unspoken,
Cool as the morning star.

# Evening Walk in France

When twilight comes, before it gets too late,
We swing behind us the heavy iron gate,

And as it clangs shut, stand a moment there
To taste the world, the larger open air,

And walk among the grandeur of the vines,
Those long rows written in imperfect lines,

Low massive trunks that bear the delicate
Insignia of leaves where grapes are set;

And here the sky is a great roofless room
Where late bees and late people wander home,

And here we walk on slowly through the dusk
And watch the long waves of the dark that mask

Black cypresses far off, and gently take
The sumptuous clouds and roofs within their wake,

Until the solid nearer haystacks seem
Like shadows looming ghostly out of dream,

And the stone farm becomes an ancient lair,
Dissolving into dusk—and is not there.

A dog barks, and a single lamp is lit.
We are two silent shadows crossing it.

Under the lamp a woman stands at rest,
Cutting a loaf of bread across her breast.

## Dutch Interior

*Pieter de Hooch* (*1629–1682*)

I recognize the quiet and the charm,
This safe enclosed room where a woman sews
And life is tempered, orderly, and calm.

Through the Dutch door, half-open, sunlight streams
And throws a pale square down on the red tiles.
The cosy black dog suns himself and dreams.

Even the bed is sheltered, it encloses,
A cupboard to keep people safe from harm,
Where copper glows with the warm flush of roses.

The atmosphere is all domestic, human,
Chaos subdued by the sheer power of need.
This is a room where I have lived as woman,

Lived too what the Dutch painter does not tell—
The wild skies overhead, dissolving, breaking,
And how that broken light is never still,

And how the roar of waves is always near,
What bitter tumult, treacherous and cold,
Attacks the solemn charm year after year!

It must be felt as peace won and maintained
Against those terrible antagonists—
How many from this quiet room have drowned?

How many left to go, drunk on the wind,
And take their ships into heartbreaking seas;
How many whom no woman's peace could bind?

Bent to her sewing, she looks drenched in calm.
Raw grief is disciplined to the fine thread.
But in her heart this woman is the storm;

Alive, deep in herself, holds wind and rain,
Remaking chaos into an intimate order
Where sometimes light flows through a windowpane.

## A Vision of Holland

The marriage of this horizontal land
Lying so low, so open and exposed,
Flat as an open palm, and never closed
To restless storm and the relentless wind,

This marriage of low land and towering air—
It took my breath away. I am still crazed
Here a month later, in my uplands, dazed
By so much light, so close to despair.

Infinite vertical! Who climbs to Heaven?
Who can assault the cloud's shimmering peak?
Here the intangible is the mystique,
No rock to conquer and no magic mountain,

Only the horizontal infinite
Stretched there below to polarize
The rush of height itself, where this land lies
Immense and still, covered by changing light.

Those troubling clouds pour through the mind.
An earthquake of pure atmosphere
Cracks open every elemental fear.
The light is passionate, but not defined.

So we are wracked as by a psychic fault,
Stormed and illuminated. "Oh sky, sky,
Earth, earth, and nothing else," we cry,
Knowing once more how absolutes exalt.

Slowly the eye comes back again to rest
There on a house, canal, cows in a field.
The visionary moment has to yield,
But the defining eye is newly blest.

Come back from that cracked-open psychic place,
It is alive to wonders freshly seen:
After the earthquake, gentle pastures green,
And that great miracle, a human face.

## Bears and Waterfalls

Kind kinderpark
For bear buffoons
And fluid graces—
Who dreamed this lark
Of spouts, lagoons,
And huge fur faces?

For bears designed
Small nooks, great crags,
And Gothic mountains?
For bears refined
Delightful snags,
Waterfalls, fountains?

Who had the wit to root
A forked tree where a sack
Of honey plumps on end,
A rich-bottomed fruit
To rouse a hearty whack
From passing friend?

Who ever did imagine
A waterspout as stool,
Or was black bear the wiser
Who sat down on this engine
To keep a vast rump cool.
Then, cooled, set free a geyser?

Who dreamed a great brown queen
Sleeked down in her rough silk
Flirting with her huge lord,
Breast-high in her tureen?—
"Splash me, delightful hulk!"
So happy and absurd.

Bear upside-down, white splendor,
All creamy, foaming fur,
And childhood's rug come true,
All nonchalance and candor,
Black pads your signature—
Who, above all, dreamed you?

When natural and formal
Are seen to mate so well,
Where bears and fountains play,
Who would return to normal?
Go back to human Hell?
Not I. I mean to stay,

To hold this happy chance
Forever in the mind,
To be where waters fall
And archetypes still dance,
As they were once designed
In Eden for us all.

## A Parrot

My parrot is emerald green,
His tail feathers, marine.
He bears an orange half-moon
Over his ivory beak.
He must be believed to be seen,
This bird from a Rousseau wood.
When the urge is on him to speak,
He becomes too true to be good.

He uses his beak like a hook
To lift himself up with or break
Open a sunflower seed,
And his eye, in a bold white ring,
Has a lapidary look.
What a most astonishing bird,
Whose voice when he chooses to sing
Must be believed to be heard.

That stuttered staccato scream
Must be believed not to seem
The shriek of a witch in the room.
But he murmurs some muffled words
(Like someone who talks through a dream)
When he sits in the window and sees
The to-and-fro wings of wild birds
In the leafless improbable trees.

## Eine Kleine Snailmusik

*The snail watchers are interested in snails from all angles. . . . At the moment they are investigating the snail's reaction to music. "We have played to them on the harp in the garden and in the country on the pipe," said Mr. Heaton, "and we have taken them into the house and played to them on the piano."*

The London Star

What soothes the angry snail?
What's music to his horn?
For the "Sonata Appassionata,"
He shows scorn,
And Handel
Makes the frail snail
Quail,
While Prokofieff
Gets no laugh,
And Tchaikovsky, I fear,
No tear.
Piano, pipe, and harp,
Dulcet or shrill,
Flat or sharp,
Indoors or in the garden,
Are willy-nilly
Silly
To the reserved, slow,
Sensitive
Snail,
Who prefers to live
Glissandissimo,
Pianissimo.

## The Fig

Under the green leaf hangs a little pouch
Shaped like a gourd, purple and leathery.
It fits the palm, it magnetizes touch.
What flesh designed as fruit can this fruit be?

The plump skin gives a little at the seam.
Now bite it deep for better or for worse!
Oh multitude of stars, pale green and crimson—
And you have dared to eat a universe!

## A Hard Death

We have seen how dignity can be torn
From the naked dying or the newly born
By a loud voice or an ungentle presence,
Harshness of haste or lack of reverence;
How the hospital nurse may casually unbind
The suffering body from the lucid mind.
The spirit enclosed in that fragile shell
Cannot defend itself, must endure all.
And not only the dying, helpless in a bed,
Ask for a little pillow for the head,
A sip of water, a cool hand to blss:
The living have their lonely agonies.
"Is there compassion?" a friend asked me.
"Does it exist in another country?"

The busy living have no time to see
The flowers, so silent and so alive,
That paling to lavender of the anemone,
That purpling of the rose no one can save,
Dying, but at each second so complete
A photograph would show no slightest change.
Only the human eye, imperfect but aware,
Knows that the flower arrested on the air
Is flying thtrough space, doing a dance
Toward the swift fall of petals, all at once.

God's Grace, given freely, we do not deserve,
But we can choose at least to see its ghost
On every face. Oh, we can wish to serve
Each other gently as we live, though lost.
We cannot save, be saved, but we can stand
Before each presence with gentle heart and hand;
Here in this place, in this time without belief,
Keep the channels open to each other's grief;
Never accept a death or life as strange
To its essence, but at each second be aware
How God is moving always through each flower
From birth to death in a multiple gesture

Of abnegation; and when the petals fall
Say it is beautiful and good, say it is well.

I saw my mother die and now I know
The spirit cannot be defended. It must go
Naked even of love at the very end.
"Take the flowers away" (Oh, she had been their friend!),
And we who ached could do nothing more—
She was detached and distant as a star.

Let us be gentle to each other this brief time
For we shall die in exile far from home,
Where even the flowers can no longer save.
Only the living can be healed by love.

## The Silence

At first the silence is a silence only,
A huge lack rather than a huge something.
I listen for a voice in this dead vacuum,
Feel destitute, abandoned, full of dread.

Season of growing light and dirty snow
When we are too vulnerable for words.

The silence—at first it is empty.
Tears fall out of my eyes like falling leaves.
To whom, to what is it good-by? Such grief.
At first the silence is a silence only.

Season of separation and the winter freeze.
Only the skies are open these hard days.

The brooks are numbed inside their caves of ice.
Who knows—who can?—what is in store for us?
Our dying planet where the glazed fields shine—
No gentle snow falls in this cruel time.

Silence, a membrane. Somehow I must get through
Into the universe where stars still flock,
To the rich world not empty but wide open,
Where soul quietly breathes and is at home.

First, I must go beyond the loneliness,
Refuse dependence and not ask for love.

So I went up the hill with my raw grief,
Found lambs there, shivering, newly born.
The sheep's gruff voice, anxious, as she licked one,
Repeated a hoarse word, a word torn from her,

I had never heard that sound before—
That throaty cry of hunger and arrival.

Oh yes, I nearly drowned with longing then . . .
Now winter hills surround me in the evening light.
A dying sun, cold sky flushed with rose
Speak of the separation in all birth.

At first the silence is a silence only . . .
But huge lack bears huge something through the dark.

## Annunciation

In this suspense of ours before the fall,
Before the end, before the true beginning,
No word, no feeling can be pure or whole.
Bear the loss first, then the infant winning;
Agony first, and then the long farewell.
So the child leaves the parent torn at birth.
No one is perfect here, no one is well:
It is a time of fear and immolation.
First the hard journey down again to death
Without a saving word or a free breath,
And then the terrible annunciation:
And we are here alone upon the earth.

The angel comes and he is always grave.
Joy is announced as if it were despair.
Mary herself could do nothing to save,
Nothing at all but to believe and bear,
Nothing not to foresee that in the ending
Would lie the true beginning and the birth,
And all be broken down before the mending.
For there can never be annunciation
Without the human heart's descent to Hell.
And no ascension without the fearful fall.
The angel's wings foretold renunciation,
And left her there alone upon the earth.

## At Chartres

Perhaps there is no smallest consolation,
No help, no saving grace, no little ease;
Only the presence of this pure compassion
We lifted up, who fall upon our knees.
Nothing we have to give it or implore.
It does not speak to us. It has no face,
And is itself only an open door—
Forever open, that will never close.

Here we are measured by our own creation.
Against this little anguish, this short breath,
Those choirs of glass rise up in an ovation,
Ourselves so small, this house so huge with faith.
Here we are measured against the perfect love,
Transparent glowing walls define and free.
The door is open, but we cannot move,
Nor be consoled or saved. But only see.

## Once More at Chartres

A desperate child, I run up to this gate
With all my fears withheld and all my dark
Contained, to breathe out in one breath
All I have carried in my heart of death,
All I have buried in my mind of hate.
Once more I stand within the ancient ark.

> Chartres, you are here who never will not be,
> Ever becoming what you always are.
> So, lifted by our human eyes, each hour,
> The arch is breathed alive into its power,
> Still being builded for us who still see
> Hands lifting stone into the perilous air.

A child, I rest in your maternal gaze,
That which encompasses and shelters, yet,
Lifting so gently, still demands rebirth,
Breaks open toward sky the dark of earth,
And proves unyielding where the rose is set,
Where Love is light itself and severe praise.

> Chartres, you the reason beyond any faith,
> The prayer we make who never learned to pray,
> The patient recreator of creation,
> O distant friend, O intimate relation,
> You living seed in the disease of death,
> And long becoming of our only day,

I stand within your arduous embrace.
This is pure majesty, there is no other.
I suffer all beginnings and all ends.
Here this enclosure opens and transcends
All weaker hopes under your tragic face—
The suffering child here must become the mother.

## Jonah

I come back from the belly of the whale
Bruised from the struggle with a living wall,
Drowned in a breathing dark, a huge heartbeat
That jolted helpless hands and useless feet,

Yet know it was not death, that vital warm,
Nor did the monster wish me any harm;
Only the prisoning was hard to bear
And three-weeks' need to burst back into air . . .

Slowly the drowned self must be strangled free
And lifted whole out of that inmost sea,
To lie newborn under compassionate sky,
As fragile as a babe, with welling eye.

Do not be anxious, for now all is well,
The sojourn over in that fluid Hell,
My heart is nourished on no more than air,
Since every breath I draw is answered prayer.

## Easter Morning

The extreme delicacy of this Easter morning
Spoke to me as a prayer and as a warning.
It was light on the brink, spring light
After a rain that gentled my dark night.
I walked through landscapes I had never seen
Where the fresh grass had just begun to green,
And its roots, watered deep, sprung to my tread;
The maples wore a cloud of feathery red,
But flowering trees still showed their clear design
Against the pale blue brightness chilled like wine.
And I was praying all the time I walked,
While starlings flew about, and talked, and talked.
Somewhere and everywhere life spoke the word.
The dead trees woke; each bush held its bird.
I prayed for delicate love and difficult,
That all be gentle now and know no fault,
That all be patient—as a wild rabbit fled
Sudden before me. Dear love, I would have said
(And to each bird who flew up from the wood),
I would be gentler still if that I could,
For on this Easter morning it would seem
The softest footfall danger is, extreme . . .
And so I prayed to be less than the grass
And yet to feel the Presence that might pass.
I made a prayer. I heard the answer, "Wait,
When all is so in peril, and so delicate!"

# The Godhead as Lynx

Kyrie Eleison, O wild lynx!
Mysterious sad eyes, and yet so bright,
Wherein mind never grieves or thinks,
But absolute attention is alight—
Before that golden gaze, so deep and cold,
My human rage dissolves, my pride is broken.
I am a child here in a world grown old.
Eons ago its final word was spoken.
Eyes of the god, hard as obsidian,
Look into mine. Kyrie Eleison.

Terrible as it is, your gaze consoles,
And awe turns tender before your guiltless head.
(What we have lost to enter into souls!)
I feel a longing for the lynx's bed,
To submerge self in that essential fur,
And sleep close to this ancient world of grace,
As if there could be healing next to her,
The mother-lynx in her prehuman place.
Yet that pure beauty does not know compassion—
O cruel god, Kyrie Eleison!

It is the marvelous world, free of our love,
Free of our hate, before our own creation,
Animal world, so still and so alive.
We never can go back to pure sensation,
Be self-possessed as the great lynx, or calm.
Yet she is lightning to cut down the lamb,
A beauty that devours without a qualm,
A cruel god who only says, "I am,"
Never, "You must become," as you, our own
God, say forever. Kyrie Eleison!

How rarely You look out from human eyes,
Yet it is we who bear creation on,
Troubled, afflicted, and so rarely wise,
Feeling nostalgia for an old world gone.
Imperfect as we are, and never whole,
Still You live in us like a fertile seed,

Always becoming, and asking of the soul
To stretch beyond sweet nature, answer need,
And lay aside the beauty of the lynx
To be this laboring self who groans and thinks.

## The Waves

Even in the middle of the silent firs,
The secret world of mushroom and of moss,
Where all is delicate and nothing stirs,
We get the rumor of those distant wars
And the harsh sound of loss.

This is an island open to the churning,
The boom, the constant cannonade,
The turning back of tides and their returning,
And ocean broken like some restless mourning
That cannot find a bed.

Oh love, let us be true then to this will—
Not to each other, human and defeated,
But to great power, our Heaven and our Hell,
That thunders out its triumph unabated,
And is never still.

For we are married to this rocky coast,
To the charge of huge waves upon it,
The ceaseless war, the tide gained and then lost,
And ledges worn down smooth but not downcast—
Wild rose and granite.

Here in the darkness of the stillest wood,
Absence, the ocean, tires us with its roar;
We bear love's thundering rumor in the blood
Beyond our understanding, ill or good—
Listen, once more!

## Beyond the Question

### 1

The phoebe sits on her nest
Hour after hour,
Day after day,
Waiting for life to burst out
From under her warmth.

Can I weave a nest for silence,
Weave it of listening,
Listening,
Layer upon layer?

But one must first become small,
Nothing but a presence,
Attentive as a nesting bird,
Proffering no slightest wish,
No tendril of a wish
Toward anything that might happen
Or be given,
Only the warm, faithful waiting,
Contained in one's smallness.

Beyond the question, the silence.
Before the answer, the silence.

### 2

When all is in order,
Flowers on each mantel,
Floors swept,
Newspapers laid aside,
Wars, deaths suspended . . .
Silence flows in
And it happens—
A patch of sunlight
On the wall, a message;
The great white peony,
An illumination.
Each thing is haloed.
I live in a Book of Hours.

### 3

Before my eyes the peony,
An arrested whirlpool,
Soft as the breast of a swan,
Floats on the air . . .

Before my eyes,
The petals fall apart,
Plop down
In shapeless confusion,
The pure form spent.

Creation itself
Tears the fabric apart,
In the instant of achievement
Makes new demands.

Must I rejoice
In the harsh, fertile
Answer to loss,
The stiff, five-pointed seed?

Not keep it
A moment longer,
Magic floating on air,
The flower,
The fulfillment?

No, creation says,
Not a moment longer.

### 4

Voices do not speak
From a cloud.
They breathe through the blood.
They are there in the stem
(Plant or human flesh).

Does the seed too resist?
But something cracks the shell,
Breaks down the pod,
Explodes

That dark enclosed life,
Safe, self-contained,
Pushes the frail root out,
The fresh dangerous leaf.

Voices do not speak
From a cloud,
But we are inhabited.

### 5

Now at last
The dialogue begins again.
I lay my cheek on the hard earth
And listen, listen.

No, it is not the endless conversations
Of the grasses and their shallow roots;
No, it is not the beetles,
The good worms, I hear
But tremor much deeper down.

Answer?
But the answer is happening,
Flows through every crevice
And across the stillest air.
Under the ledges
Artesian water
Flows fast
Even in time of drought.

## Invocation

Come out of the dark earth
Here where the minerals
Glow in their stone cells
Deeper than seed or birth.

Come under the strong wave
Here where the tug goes
As the tide turns and flows
Below that architrave.

Come into the pure air
Above all heaviness
Of storm and cloud to this
Light-possessed atmosphere.

Come into, out of, under
The earth, the wave, the air.
Love, touch us everywhere
With primeval candor.

# A Durable Fire
# (1969–1972)

# Gestalt at Sixty

## 1

For ten years I have been rooted in these hills,
The changing light on landlocked lakes,
For ten years have called a mountain, friend,
Have been nourished by plants, still waters,
Trees in their seasons,
Have fought in this quiet place
For my *self*.

I can tell you that first winter
I heard the trees groan.
I heard the fierce lament
As if they were on the rack under the wind.
I too have groaned here,
Wept the wild winter tears.
I can tell you that solitude
Is not all exaltation, inner space
Where the soul breathes and work can be done.
Solitude exposes the nerve,
Raises up ghosts.
The past, never at rest, flows through it.

Who wakes in a house alone
Wakes to moments of panic.
(Will the roof fall in?
Shall I die today?)
Who wakes in a house alone
Wakes to inertia sometimes,
To fits of weeping for no reason.
Solitude swells the inner space
Like a balloon.
We are wafted hither and thither
On the air currents.
How to land it?

I worked out anguish in a garden.
Without the flowers,
The shadow of trees on snow, their punctuation,
I might not have survived.

I came here to create a world
As strong, renewable, fertile,
As the world of nature all around me—
Learned to clear myself as I have cleared the pasture,
Learned to wait,
Learned that change is always in the making
(Inner and outer) if one can be patient,
Learned to trust myself.


2


The house is receptacle of a hundred currents.
Letters pour in,
Rumor of the human ocean, never at rest,
Never still. . . .
Sometimes it deafens and numbs me.

I did not come here for society
In these years
When every meeting is collision,
The impact huge,
The reverberations slow to die down.
Yet what I have done here
I have not done alone,
Inhabited by a rich past of lives,
Inhabited also by the great dead,
By music, poetry—
Yeats, Valéry stalk through this house.
No day passes without a visitation—
Rilke, Mozart.
I am always a lover here,
Seized and shaken by love.

Lovers and friends,
I come to you starved
For all you have to give,
Nourished by the food of solitude,
A good instrument for all you have to tell me,
For all I have to tell you.
We talk of first and last things,
Listen to music together,

Climb the long hill to the cemetery
In autumn,
Take another road in spring
Toward newborn lambs.

No one comes to this house
Who is not changed.
I meet no one here who does not change me.

### 3

How rich and long the hours become,
How brief the years,
In this house of gathering,
This life about to enter its seventh decade.

I live like a baby
Who bursts into laughter
At a sunbeam on the wall,
Or like a very old woman
Entranced by the prick of stars
Through the leaves.

And now, as the fruit gathers
All the riches of summer
Into its compact world,
I feel richer than ever before,
And breathe a larger air.

I am not ready to die,
But I am learning to trust death
As I have trusted life.
I am moving
Toward a new freedom
Born of detachment,
And a sweeter grace—
Learning to let go.

I am not ready to die,
But as I approach sixty
I turn my face toward the sea.
I shall go where tides replace time,
Where my world will open to a far horizon

Over the floating, never-still flux and change.
I shall go with the changes,
I shall look far out over golden grasses
And blue waters. . . .

There are no farewells.

Praise God for His mercies,
For His austere demands,
For His light
And for His darkness.

## Myself to Me

"Set the table and sweep the floor—
Love will not come back to this door.

Plant your bulbs, sow summer flowers.
These be your joys, these your powers.

A cat for comfort, wood to burn,
And changing light as seasons turn.

Long hours alone and work to do—
These are your strength. These are for you."

So spoke myself. I listened well;
I thought that self had truth to tell.

But love came back after many a year,
Love all unasked knocked at the door,

Love all unasked broke down the door,
To bring me pain as it did before,

To bring me back lost poetry,
And all I'd meant alone to be.

What does myself now say to me?
"Open the door to Mystery.

Gather the grapes from any vine,
And make rich wine, and make rich wine.

Out of the passion comes the form,
And only passion keeps it warm.

Set the table, sweep the floor—
Forget the lies you told before."

## Dear Solid Earth

Dear solid earth after ambiguous seas!
Oh gentle sand, incarnate mystery,
The body all at rest!

I battled waves, the depths of black and green,
Almost went down, heavy with death alone,
Now comforted and blest.

Good-by to dangerous undertows, dispelled
For this calm wisdom never to be told
Where two souls melt.

We lie now all forgiven and enclosed
After the dispersed years when we supposed
All had been lost—and felt.

The nearly drowned, exhausted swimmer lies,
A shell in her clasped hand, salt in her eyes,
On this strange friendly shore.

It is enough simply to breathe again,
To breath an easy long breath after pain,
Nor ask for more.

## The Return of Aphrodite

Under the wave it is altogether still,
Alive and still, as nourishing as sleep,
Down below conflict, beyond need or will,
Where love flows on and yet is there to keep,
As unconstrained as waves that lift and break
And their bright foam neither to give nor take.

Listen to the long rising curve and stress,
Murmur of ocean that brings us the goddess.

From deep she rises, poised upon her shell.
Oh guiltless Aphrodite so long absent!
The green waves part. There is no sound at all
As she advances, tranquil and transparent,
To lay on mortal flesh her sacred mantle.

The wave recedes—she is drawn back again
Into the ocean where light leaves a stain.

## Inner Space

We reach the area of no more hiding,
An inner space as open as the palm.
This is no ambience of childish confiding,
Exchange of lives, however great that charm.
Where we live now is far more exposed,
Not even to each other's need or gift,
But to the region love has proposed,
Open as a huge sky where planets lift,
Mysterious order, all shining and all clear—
No ambiguity to be refined
In a neurotic, dangerous atmosphere.
All is new here. We are to be defined.
We come together in an inner space
As rigorous, as deep as outer space.

## Things Seen

A bluebird sudden as the flash of thought,
Embodied azure never to be caught.

The flowing white-on-white transparency
Of light through petals of a peony.

The shining ripple through tall meadow grass
Under the wind's invisible caress.

Unshadowed, vulnerable, smiling peace
Caught in one glance at a sleeping face.

Within love's new-sprung, light-shot, vivid green
My eyes are open. Angels can be seen.

They come and go as natural as you please—
What stirs? What wing there in the silent trees?

## Mozart Again

Now it is Mozart who comes back again
All garlanded in green.
Flute, harp, and trumpet, the sweet violin—
Each sound is seen.

Spring is a phrase, repeated green refrain,
Sound of new leaves springing.
I see the wind flowing like slanted rain,
Wind winging.

I learn this loving fresh, in ancient style
(Lightly time flows),
And mine a green world for pure joy awhile.
Listen, a rose!

Leaves are glissando. A long haunting phrase
Ripples the air—
This harpsichord of light that the wind plays.
Mozart is there.

## The Tree Peony

The old tree peony I had almost given up
Today presented a huge single flower.
Slowly, one by one, white petals,
Serrated, translucent,
Opened to the shaggy golden crown
At the heart.
My green world stood still
Around that presence,
Godlike, gathering the light.

How innocent the flesh that is born again
Like some awesome flower the Chinese sages
Devote a lifetime to contemplate and render,
Or I in my garden wait four years to see—
The pristine act of loving and being loved!

## A Chinese Landscape

I drove home through the morning, rich and still,
Where cloudy dragons floated every hill,
And winding rivers glittered and were lost
In the green haze of trees and rising mist,
The earth enfolded all around and blest
By autumn light, the fertile earth at rest.

As rich and gentled I after this harvest
Where every power fulfilled has come to rest,
And passionate love has learned a quiet ease
Like rivers winding through lyrical trees,
In time as spacious as early autumn light
When the mists rise and all is calm and bright.

For the first time I left you without woe,
So filled with wisdom I could even go
Holding our love at rest within my mind,
A Chinese painting where rich rivers wind
And lovers on a bridge over a small ravine
With their sole presence focus the huge scene.

## Reeds and Water

We look out, dazzled, at a shining lake
And up at light under long branches flowing
Along the silvery bark, a supple snake,
And leaves still dappled green before their going.

The background, ragged trees at water's edge,
But close at hand the pointed reeds define
And punctuate the glitter, a black wedge
That gives the casual scene a firm design.

Water and reeds—pure joy ran its course,
Compelling joy that drew us home, who now
Recapture the same light and feel its force
Flowing under the flesh as if a bough.

Reeds and still water—what better image spoken
For us, these autumn lovers, who must part
Over and over, the moment's shining broken,
Only to feel light flow back through the heart?

## The Snow Light

In the snow light,
In the swan light,
In the white-on-white light
Of a winter storm,
My delight and your delight
Kept each other warm.

The next afternoon—
And love gone so soon!—
I met myself alone
In a windless calm,
Silenced at the bone
After the white storm.

What more was to come?
Out from the cocoon,
In the silent room,
Pouring out white light,
Amaryllis bloom
Opened in the night.

The cool petals shone
Like some winter moon
Or shadow of a swan,
Echoing the light
After you were gone
Of our white-on-white.

## Warning

Now, in the brilliant sun,
In the winter cold,
Under this blazing sky,
We have had warning.
No one escapes. No one.
The brilliant young grow old.
The heart's frightening cry
Is heard at borning.
Accept, remember: all,
Even strong trees, die.
The whole world's burning.

Now in the brilliant day,
In the living blue,
Under this tent of Now,
We grasp hard truth,
Grasp it, not turn away—
You too, beloved you.
Because today I know,
Don't speak to me of death,
But speak to me. Write often—
Your work, your joy, the snow.
Warm me with your breath.

## Surfers

Now we are balanced
On the high tide of the hour
Taking the wave with ease
As it breaks under us,
The tug and heave under our feet,
Flowing with, poised on
The dangerous power—
Experienced surfers who can ride it.

And then the landing,
To heave a heavy board
Onto hard wet sand,
The change of elements
We learn again at every parting
When we lie alone
And feel the long reverberation
Slowly dying down.

I have fought impermanence and change,
All my life tried to hold time still;
Now I must learn a new thing—
To take parting like a surfer,
Resume myself alone on the sand,
No rider now, a contemplative,
Permitting love its eloquent changes,
Glad to have ridden the big waves,
Glad to be very quiet now.

## All Day I Was with Trees

Across wild country on solitary roads
Within a fugue of parting, I was consoled
By birches' sovereign whiteness in sad woods,
Dark glow of pines, a single elm's distinction—
I was consoled by trees.

In February we see the structure change—
Or the light change, and so the way we see it.
Tensile and delicate, the trees stand now
Against the early skies, the frail fresh blue,
In an attentive stillness.

Naked, the trees are singularly present,
Although their secret force is still locked in.
Who could believe that the new sap is rising
And soon we shall draw up amazing sweetness
From stark maples?

All day I was with trees, a fugue of parting,
All day I lived in long cycles, not brief hours.
A tenderness of light before new falls of snow
Lay on the barren landscape like a promise.
Love nourished every vein.

## A Storm of Angels

Anarchic anger came to beat us down,
Until from all that battering we went numb
Like ravaged trees after a hurricane.
But in its wake we saw fierce angels come—
Not gentle and not kind—who threshed the grain
With their harsh wings, winnowed from waste.
They brought love to its knees in fearful pain.
Such angels come after the storm is past
As messengers of a true power denied.
They beat us down. For love, they thrash us free,
Down to the truth itself, stripped of our pride.
On those harsh winds they bring us agony.
Theirs is an act of grace, and it is given
To those in Hell who can imagine Heaven.

## The Angels and the Furies

*Ange plein de gaîté connaissez-vous l'angoisse?*
Baudelaire

### 1

Have you not wounded yourself
And battered those you love
By sudden motions of evil,
Black rage in the blood
When the soul, *premier danseur*,
Spins toward a murderous fall?
The furies possess you.

### 2

Have you not surprised yourself
Sometimes by sudden motions
Or intimations of goodness,
When the soul, *premier danseur*,
Perfectly poised,
Could shower blessings
With a graceful turn of the head?
The angels are there.

### 3

The angels, the furies
Are never far away
While we dance, we dance,
Trying to keep a balance,
To be perfectly human
(Not perfect, never perfect,
Never an end to growth and peril),
Able to bless and forgive
Ourselves.
This is what is asked of us.

### 4

It is light that matters,
The light of understanding.

Who has ever reached it
Who has not met the furies again and again?
Who has reached it without
Those sudden acts of grace?

## After an Island

What the child saw with dazzled eyes
And ran to meet
In a fury of exploration—
The radiant skies,
Blue over blue, blue over green,
Blue over white sand,
Changing light, clouds,
Shells, birds,
Sand under bare feet,
Sun on chilled skin,
And the plunge into lucid green
Beyond the broken wave
Dragging its treasure . . .

What the child plundered
With eyes, mouth, hands,
We bring home now
With a handful of shells
To sort and think over.
What can we discard
From an island week?
What can we keep?
What happened there?

All that we shared
Must be free to roam,
Not held too close,
Given to the singular mind
To explore alone
In that deep place
Where the sensuous image
Marries the soul.

Now it is the intermittent descent
Of roseate wings
As, one by one,
The spoonbills float down—
At sunset, rose against rose—
To rest on still water.

Now the sudden vision,
Explosive,
Of the sharp red crest,
The staccato hammer
Of the pileated woodpecker.

Now the solitary hawk at dusk,
His great presence
Ominous, intense,
Watching.

Now the flittering, darting
Of shore birds in and out of the foam,
The sharp practical eyes,
The swift, skittering legs.

This is an Easter
Of the intensely visual
Translated to the inmost being,
Where we shall learn (perhaps)
To float the mind as if on wings,
Supported by currents of memory
Above the thickets of all that stops the flow
Between us,
Our disparate lives.

Apart, we meet on these calm memories,
Among essences and absolutes—
Long draughts of sky,
Attentive looks
At the detail of bill, webbed foot,
Or small black line
Above a warbler's eye.
An Easter strangely bare
Of our human sorrow,
Complexity, iriritations;
Love this time
Wind-threshed, wave-beaten
To impersonal joy.

After the fervor,
This new detachment.

Hold them in balance
And we come to the wisdom
That says "forever,"
To the Easter of human love,
Or, if you will, an island.

## Fulfillment

We hold it in our keeping, even apart,
Twin trees whose pollen has been swiftly crossed,
And all this sumptuous flowering of the heart
Will grow rich fruit, nor anything be lost.

Fall, petals, fall, cover the green with snow!
There is no grieving loss, and no alarm.
The palaces of leaves begin to show
The small fruit swelling in the summer calm.

So grave a state of being holds us still
There at the center where the roots drink deep.
The leaves may tremble but the winds fulfill
The autumn fruit, knotting when flowers sleep.

There is no place for yearning, we must grow.
We live now in the heart of Mystery,
Part of Creation's deepest urge and flow
To which bears witness every flower and tree.

## The Autumn Sonnets

### 1

Under the leaves an infant love lies dead,
But we will have no mourning. It is good.
This was the useless crying in my head.
This was the grieving fury in my blood.
The house is being buried—so it seems—
Under the brittle trash of leaves let go,
The infant anguish and the infant dreams,
Soon to be lost forever under snow,
While sleeping beauty sleeps toward a spring
When Love, the prince, will come back through the green
As once he did when time was on the wing,
And he will push aside a flowery screen
To wake a woman, full-grown, rich in light,
Whose infant cries were stilled one autumn night.

### 2

If I can let you go as trees let go
Their leaves, so casually, one by one;
If I can come to know what they do know,
That fall is the release, the consummation,
Then fear of time and the uncertain fruit
Would not distemper the great lucid skies
This strangest autumn, mellow and acute.
If I can take the dark with open eyes
And call it seasonal, not harsh or strange
(For love itself may need a time of sleep),
And, treelike, stand unmoved before the change,
Lose what I lose to keep what I can keep,
The strong root still alive under the snow,
Love will endure—if I can let you go.

### 3

I wake to gentle mist over the meadow,
The chilling atmosphere before sunrise
Where half my world lies still asleep in shadow
And half is touched awake as if by eyes.

Sparse yellow leaves high in the air are struck
To sudden flame as the first rays break through
And all the brightness gathers to that mark,
While floating in the dim light far below
A monarch settles on an autumn crocus
For one last drink before impending flight.
The slow pulse of the wings brings into focus
The autumn scene and all its dark and bright,
And suddenly the granite rock is split
As sun lights up exactly half of it.

### 4

I never thought that it could be, not once,
The Muse appearing in warm human guise,
She the mad creature of unhappy chance
Who looked at me with cold Medusa eyes,
Giver of anguish and so little good.
For how could I have dreamed that you would come
To help me tame the wildness in my blood,
To bring the struggling poet safely home?
The grand design is clear, but we must work
To make it viable. The vision presses,
And I have never doubted its true mark
Where all I suffer stems from all that blesses;
For what I know, both vulnerable and great,
Is Love, that prince, who teaches me to wait.

### 5

After a night of rain the brilliant screen
Below my terraced garden falls away.
And there, far off, I see the hills again
On this, a raw and windy, somber day.
Moment of loss, and it is overwhelming
(Crimson and gold gone, that rich tapestry),
But a new vision, quiet and soul-calming,
Distance, design, are given back to me.
This is good poverty, now love is lean,
More honest, harder than it ever was
When all was glamoured by a golden screen.

The hills are back, and silver on the grass,
As I look without passion or despair
Out on a larger landscape, grand and bare.

### 6

As if the house were dying or already dead;
As if nobody cared—and, in fact, who does?
(Whose feet but mine wear out the painted tread?
Who listens for the fly's autumnal buzz?
Who climbs the stair to a wide upstairs bed?);
As if the house were prepared every day
By an odd owner with madness in her head
For visitors who never come to stay,
For love that has no time here or elsewhere,
Who keeps fresh flowers on each mantel still,
And sweeps the hearth and warms the chilling air
As if to keep the house alive on will—
Truth is, her daily battle is with death,
Back to the wall and fighting for each breath.

### 7

Twice I have set my heart upon a sharing,
Twice have imagined a real human home,
Having forgotten how some fiercer caring
Demands this naked solitude for loam.
Now love pours out in light from every wound
I know the kind of home this cannot be,
And know more savagely what I have found—
An open door into great mystery.
I came here first for haven from despair
And found a deeper root than passionate love,
A wilder inscape and a safer lair
Where the intrinsic being kept alive.
Home is a granite rock and two sparse trees
As light and shadow may inhabit these.

### 8

I ponder it again and know for sure
My life has asked not love but poetry,

Asked less for joy than power to endure.
More than ten years this house has sheltered me.
The challenge never changed. It always was
What I could make out of sheer deprivation,
The falling leaf, the silver on the grass,
Sometimes a piercing moment of sensation
As when I look out into autumn haze
And catch under the apple a young buck
To meet his long attentive fearless gaze.
The rest has been work and a little luck,
Keeping the balance between loneliness
And the dark heart of silence that can bless.

## 9

This was our testing year after the first
When we were drunk on love and drunk on light.
Unquenchable our hunger and our thirst
For shining presence through the longest night.
Somehow we wrote each other every day,
Mingled disparate lives in rich exchange.
All must be now. What if it did not stay?
All must be tightly held for fear of change.
But such fierce ardor soon wore itself out.
The phone became a monstrous instrument,
And words tangled themselves into a knot.
Something got frayed of all we felt and meant.
It was the year of testing. Now we know
Exactly what was asked: we had to grow.

## 10

We watched the waterfalls, rich and baroque,
As a bright stream flowed into an impasse
And there exploded over jagged rock
In shining sheaves as if of liquid glass.
Within the roar no spoken word could fall.
We were enclosed by water, rock, and tree,
And carried far outside the personal
To rest on primal force and symmetry.
Across turbulent water and still air

A gold leaf floated slowly past.
Our eyes, open to all that we can share,
Gave us the luminous design at rest.
We stood together in its clarity,
Because, being together, we could see.

### 11

For steadfast flame wood must be seasoned,
And if love can be trusted to last out,
Then it must first be disciplined and reasoned
To take all weathers, absences, and doubt.
No resinous pine for this, but the hard oak
Slow to catch fire, would see us through a year.
We learned to temper words before we spoke,
To force the furies back, learned to forbear,
In silence to wait out erratic storm,
And bury tumult when we were apart.
The fires were banked to keep a winter warm
With heart of oak instead of resinous heart,
And in this testing year beyond desire
Began to move toward durable fire.

## February Days

Who could tire of the long shadows,
The long shadows of the trees on snow?
Sometimes I stand at the kitchen window
For a timeless time in a long daze
Before these reflected perpendiculars,
Noting how the light has changed,
How tender it is now in February
When the shadows are blue not black.

The crimson cyclamen has opened wide,
A bower of petals drunk on the light,
And in the snow-bright ordered house
I am drowsy as a turtle in winter,
Living on light and shadow
And their changes.

## Note to a Photographer

For some months now I have lived
With that pale blue eye of spring—
A pond deep in a brown world,
Bare ground, lines of young fruit trees
Not yet in leaf.
Shining like a fish scale
In the earthy world
It gathers all the light there is.

Your pocket of sky, Photographer,
Has accompanied the winter mood,
A discreet promise
Where my anxious eye
Comes to rest on hope.

## March in New England

Here in New England where the ice still grips
And pussy willows have not put on fur,
The masts are earthbound of the sleeping ships,
And only clammers on the beaches stir.
All seems exhausted by its own withholding,
Its own withstanding. There is no unfolding.
Even the new moon promises no better
Than a thin joke about much colder weather.

This harsh world locks itself up in the season.
It is clearly not the time and not the place
To ask for summer love, for more than reason,
To hope to lift the cloud from any face.
Look at the trees, how even they determine
To hold their leaves back under the tough skin.
"Keep snug" is their advice, and they endure,
For frost is on the way again for sure.

Yet in New England before spring I've seen
The sea unfold as sumptuous as silk,
Have watched the cold world tilt back into green,
And watched the waves spill out like foaming milk—
Till the eye, starved for color and for light,
Wept at such majesty beside such blight,
Would rush to break trees open, and to bring
To this locked world torrents of English spring!

## Composition

Here is the pond, here sky, and the long grasses
That lean over the water, a slow ripple
Under the slightest wandering air that passes
To shift the scene, translating flat to stipple
On still blue water and troubling the green masses.

Three elements are spaced and subtly joined
To rest the restless mind and lift us where
Nothing in us is baffled or constrained,
Who wake and sleep as casual as they are,
And contain earth, and water, and the wind.

Take blue; take green; take the pale gold sand;
Take the slow changing shimmer of the air;
Take a huge sky above a steadfast land;
Take love, the tiger ocean in its lair,
And gentle it like grass under the wind.

## Burial

The old man who had dug the small pit
Opened the two boxes with a penknife
And let the ashes fall down into it,
The ashes of this husband and his wife,
My father and my mother gently laid
Into the earth and mingled there for good.

We watched the wind breathe up an ashen breath
And blow thin smoke along the grass—
And that was all: the bitterness of death
Lifted to air, laid in the earth. All was
Terribly silent where four people stood
Tall in the air, believing what they could.

## Of Grief

You thought it heartless
When my father fell down
Dead in his splendid prime,
Strong as a green oak thrown,
That all I did was praise
Death for this kindness,
Sang with a voice unbroken
Of the dear scholar's days,
His passion of a lifetime—
And my loss never spoken.

Judge of another's grief?
Weigh out that grief in tears?
I did not weep my father,
The rich, the fulfilled years.
What slow death have you known?
When no hope or belief
Can help, no loving care?
We watch and weep alone.
My heart broke for my mother.
I buried grief with her.

It is the incomplete,
The unfulfilled, the torn
That haunts our nights and days
And keeps us hunger-born.
Grief spills from our eyes,
Unwelcome, indiscreet,
As if sprung from a fault
As rivers seam a rock
And break through under shock.
We are shaken by guilt.

There are some griefs so loud
They could bring down the sky,
And there are griefs so still
None knows how deep they lie,
Endured, never expended.
There are old griefs so proud

They never speak a word;
They never can be mended.
And these nourish the will
And keep it iron-hard.

## Prisoner at a Desk

It is not so much trying to keep alive
As trying to keep from blowing apart
From inner explosions every day.
I sit here, open to psychic changes,
Living myself as if I were a land,
Or mountain weather, the quick cycles
Where we are tossed from the ice age
To bursts of spring, to sudden torrents
Of rain like tears breaking through iron.
It is all I can do to keep tethered down.

No prisoner at a desk, but an ocean
Or forest where waves and gentle leaves
And strange wild beasts under the groves
And whales in all their beauty under the blue
Can gently rove together, still untamed,
Where all opens and breathes and can grow.

Whatever I have learned of good behavior
Withers before these primal powers.
Here at the center governess or censor
No longer has command. The soul is here,
Inviolable splendor that exists alone.

Prisoner at a desk? No, universe of feeling
Where everything is seen, and nothing mine
To plead with or possess, only partake of,
As if at times I could put out a hand
And touch the lion head, the unicorn.
Here there is nothing, no one, not a sound
Except the distant rumor, the huge cloud
Of archetypal images that feed me . . .

Look, there are finches at the feeder.
My parrot screams with fear at a cloud.
Hyacinths are budding. Light is longer.

## Birthday Present

Renewal cannot be picked
Like a daffodil
In a swift gesture,
Cannot be cut like a pussy willow
And brought into the house.
It cannot even be imagined
Like the blue sky
We have not seen for days.

But we can be helped toward it.
True love gave me time,
Gave me, for myself alone,
This whole open day
We would have spent together.

True love gave me this—
Harder to find
Than a hummingbird's nest,
Rare as the elusive
Scent of arbutus
Under sodden leaves,
More welcome than a cup
Of spring water
After long drought.

I hold it in my hands,
I breathe it in,
I drink it,
While fifty-nine years
Of ardor and tenderness,
Of struggle and creation—
The whole complex bundle—
Falls away in a streak of light
Like a shooting star,
As the soul,
Unemcumbered,
Alive, ageless,
Meets the pristine moment:
Poetry again.

## Elegy for Louise Bogan

The death of this poet hurts us terribly,
As if a planet sank down through the sky.

Just so she was remote, just so she shone.
Singular light has gone now she is gone.

Where are they now, the aqueous green eyes,
Her violent heart, her innocent surprise?

How shall we live without her ironies
That kept her crystal clear and made us wise?

Louise, Louise, why did you have to go
In this hard time of wind and shrouding snow,

When even trees are strange and much too still,
And absence on us like some psychic chill?

We cannot have you back, but you are there,
A shining presence on our ghostly air,

Wherever soul meets soul on this dark plain
And we are worth your clarifying pain.

Deprived, distraught, often despairing,
You kneaded a celestial bread for sharing.

I have not wept a tear, nor shall I do,
Stripped to this naked praise that shines for you.

*February 10, 1970*

# Letters to a Psychiatrist

*Christmas Letter, 1970*

## 1

These bulbs forgotten in a cellar,
Pushing up through the dark their wan white shoots,
Trying to live—their hopeless hope
Has been with me like an illness
The image of what tries to be born
For twenty years or more,
But dies for lack of light.

Today I saw it again in the stare
Of the homeless cat, that hunger
Not for food only, but to be taken in,
And to trust enough to risk it . . .
Shelter, life itself. Can I tame her?
Come the worst cold, will she freeze?

How marvelous to know you can save,
Restore, nourish the abandoned,
That the life line is there
In your wise hands, Marynia!

## 2

"Yes," you say, "of course at Christmas
Half the world is suicidal."
And you are there. You answer the phone—
The wry voice with laughter in it.
Again and again the life line is thrown out.
There is no end to the work of salvage
In the drowning high seas of Christmas
When loneliness, in the name of Christ
(That longing!), attacks the world.

## 3

One by one, they come from their wilderness
Like shy wild animals
Weeping blood from their wounds,

Wounds they dare not look at
And cannot bind or heal alone.

What is it that happens then
In the small closed room
Where someone listens,
Where someone answers,
Where someone cares,
Whom they cannot hurt
With their sharp infant teeth,
With their sharp old antlers?

What does she do,
This doctor, this angel,
Who holds so many
In her human hands?
How does she heal the animal pain
So the soul may live?

4

No Ceres, she, no Aphrodite;
She cannot provide the harvest
Nor the longed-for love.

This angel must be anarchic,
Fierce, full of laughter,
Will neither punish
Nor give absolution,
Is always acute, sometimes harsh.
Still the impersonal wing
Does shelter, provides a place, a climate
Where the soul can meet itself at last.

There is no way out,
Only the way deeper and deeper inward.
There are no solutions,
But every word is action,
As is every silence.
On a good day the patient
Has used his reason
To cut through secret evasions,

Secret fears,
Has experienced himself
As a complex whole.

But angels do not operate
By any means we can define.
They come when they are needed.
(I can tell you of the resonance,
The beat of wings
Threshing out truth
Long after the hour is past.)
When they have gone
The light-riddled spirit
Is as alone as ever,
But able to fly its course again
Through the most hostile sky.

### 5

I know what it is like, Marynia.
Once I watched a jay flopping, helpless,
In the snow outside this window—
I brought it in, managed to pull out the quill
Shot through just under the eye.
I know what it is to have to be brutal
Toward the badly crippled
In order to set them free.
Then it was Easter and I saw the jay
Fly off whole into the resurrected air.

Now it is Christmas
When infant love, vulnerable beyond our knowing,
Is born again to save the world.

And for whatever crucifixions it will suffer.
Angel, be blessed for your wings.

### The Fear of Angels

It is not what they intend,
But we are light-struck,
Blinded by their presence,
When all they want is to *see* us.

We have to turn away,
Cannot look at the huge, deep Unknown
That speaks through their eyes.
They strip us down to the infant gaze
Still deep in the sky,
Still rooted somewhere we cannot remember.

Angel, look away.
I cannot afford to yield the last defense,
To go back—

"Not back, but deeper,"
Said the angel, folding his wings
To wait.

### The Action of Therapy

#### 1

After the whirlwind when all things
Were blown out of their courses
In the fiery gust,
After the whirlwind when all beams were crossed
And passionate love confused,
Its clear path lost,
Where nothing fused,
But all was burned and forced,
The psyche nearly cracked
Under the blast,
After the earthquake passed

How did it happen
That cool eyes looked out
On darkness and the storm
And cut the ties
That meant chaos and harm
So that true mysteries
Might act and charm
The haunted spirit back
To its own realm?

What did the angel do
To make all levels straight

Within that sheaf
Of troubled sense and fear,
Set every beam on its own path
At last untangled,
Singular and bright,
So that nothing was lost,
No slightest hope
Was blurred by childish grief
Outside its scope,
But all was still and clear,
So still and bright
No galaxy of stars
Could shine more absolute
On winter night?

### 2

I watched the psychic surgeon,
Stern, skilled, adroit,
Cut deep into the heart
And yet not hurt.
I watched it happen—
Old failures, old obsessions
Cut away
So blood could flow
A clear course through
Choked arteries again.
There was no pain.
My eyes, wide open,
Watched every move
In absolute surrender
To superior power.
I saw it happen
In one luminous hour
(No anesthetic given),
An act of extreme grace
And sovereign love.
From Hell I entered Heaven
And bowed my head,

Where nothing had been suffered,
But all given.

### 3

Simple acceptance
Of things as they are;
Finished, that strained arc,
Leap of the salmon upstream
Climbing waterfalls,
Sublimation
Of one death or another,
The cruel ascension
Toward loss.

Now things as they are—
Spring of the fern as it uncoils,
Brute rock broken
To show the crystal,
Light-shot February skies—
All, all have been given
After the whirlwind.

This is no repetition
Of unresolved attachments
And deprivations,
No turn of the old wheel.
It is altogether new.

### 4

In the terrifying whirlwind
When the mother is resurrected
(How many times, angelic doctor,
How many times?)
Every defense against grief goes.
There is no future,
Only excruciating repetition
Of the unburied past.
For the last time
I was torn to pieces

By my mother's anguish,
Unattainable goddess
Whose compassionate eyes
Understood me so well—
And took my heart.

I do not have to love you
As I loved her,
To be devastated, but,
Angel and surgeon of the psyche,
I am free to love you now
Outside all the myths,
The confused dreams,
Beyond all the barriers,
In the warm natural light
Of simple day.
I am allowed to give you
Unstrained, flowing,
Wise-infant
To wise-mother love.

You broke the spell;
You with your whippets around you
Like some lady in a tapestry
Said to the unicorn,
"If the child needs the mother,
The mother needs the child."
So be it.

5

In middle age we starve
For ascension,
Look back to childhood teachers
But have outgrown them.
Mature love needs new channels.
How long has it been—
What starving years—
Since I was permitted
To cherish wisdom?

I bend tenderly
Toward the young
With open heart and hands.
I share in a great love
With my equal.
Every day I learn better
About how to give
And how to receive love.
But there is still the need
To be filial toward someone,
To be devoted,
Humble and enlightened.
I need to remain teachable
For one who can teach me.
With you all green things flourish,
All flowers may be freely given,
All fears can be expressed,
No childish need is sneered at,
No adult gift unrecognized.

Speak to me
Of the communion of saints
On earth.

6

Light cannot be described,
Is nothing in itself,
Transforms all it touches.
The flower becomes transparent flame.
A plain white wall
Is marbled by flowing water,
And in the soul's realm
Light defines feeling,
Makes distinctions.

In the light
Of this penetrating mind,
Vivid response,
Total awareness,
I find myself

In a new landscape—
Fra Angelico's Paradise
(It was dear to my mother
I suddenly remember)
Where souls, released at last,
Dance together
On the simple grass.

Look, there is an owl in the tree;
A fling of lambs in February snow.
There is a donkey waving her long ears.
There is a child
With flowers in her hands.

There is a continuum
(Those garlands of joined dancers)
Of redemptive love.

I'll keep it
For a million years.

### I Speak of Change

Tumult as deep and formal as in dance
Seizes me now for every scheduled hour.
I meet you at the marrow of your power,
The Hindu *darshan*, action by pure presence.
The room is filled with words, but what I hear
Is silence growing gently like a plant
And that real space around us what I want,
The space where subtle change is drawing near.
I speak of influence as a navigator
Reckons upon the influence of a star—
Now, for a time, the light is where you are.
As the earth turns, it will be darker later.
I speak of change that cannot yet be spoken
As of a circle that will gently close
(When time and distance break the bond between us)
And will complete itself as it is broken,
So rich and rounded these ultimate hours
Where being more than love between us flowers.

### *Easter 1971*

I, in my winter poverty, alone,
Celebrate riches, come to this Easter
Humbler than I have ever been,
Closer to all that answers solitude—
The light, birds' wings, perfect silence
Of windless star-illuminated nights,
Even a sudden April storm of snow.
"Preposterous" you say about the road agent
Who has not ploughed you out this time,
And then your vivid anger turns to laughter.
Preposterous your power to enhance and probe
Whatever life may bring, your mixture
Of fervor and detachment, those antiphonies
Where the soul of a poet feeds and rests.

Preposterous your power to harmonize
And bring to its fruition the poet's gift,
Always dependent on some human eye,
On one who *sees* (never mind feeling).

Alone, without hope of being otherwise,
I come to this Easter newly rich and free
In all my gifts. I do not need your eyes
To know that we are close to an epiphany.

Fervor, detachment meet as life meets art.
There will be no tangible loss when we part,
For this epiphany is flowering from acceptance
Of a structured, impersonal, and holy dance.

### *The Contemplation of Wisdom*

To contemplate this human wisdom,
To contemplate this presence as it acts,
Slowly unraveling the mystery of pain,
Has been a task both joyful and severe.

Partaking wisdom, I have been given
The sum of many difficult acts of grace,
A vital fervor disciplined to patience.

This cup holds grief and balm in equal measure,
Light, darkness. Who drinks from it must change.

Wisdom can only give when someone takes.
To take you I go deeper into darkness
Than I could dare until this crucial year.
To take you I must take myself to judgment,
Accepting what can never be fulfilled—
My life, at best, poised on a knife-edge
Between what art would ask and what life takes;
Yet I am lavish with riches made from loss.
I summon up fresh courage from your courage.

Before we part, give me your love.
I'll use it as the key to solitude.

# Index of First Lines

A bluebird sudden as the flash of thought, 369
A charm of columns crowd, 116
A desperate child, I ran up to this gate, 349
Absorbed in planting bulbs, that work of hope, 277
Across the darkness and the silent air, 120
Across wild country on solitary roads, 377
After a night of driving rain, the skies, 207
After a night of rain the brilliant screen, 386
After the laboring birth, the clean stripped hull, 193
After the palaces, 233
After the whirlwind when all things, 403
All was dingy and dull in late afternoon, 282
Always it happens when we are not there—, 305
An early morning island, 255
An hour ago that birch, that pine, 303
An infant boy, 232
Anarchic anger came to beat us down, 378
And this too was Greece, 256
Angels, beautiful pauses in the whirlwind, 223
Anguish is always there, lurking at night, 316
As I look out on the long swell of fields, 206
As if the house were dying or already dead, 387
As it is brought in with its coat, 135

At first the silence is a silence only, 346
At first we sat imprisoned in this place, 291
At Oiso, 229
At sixty-five said, "I fight every day, 87
At the bottom of the green field she lies, 102

Beautiful is this day that brings us home, 195
Because what I want most is permanence, 137
Before we could call, 224
Boa constrictor, 232
"But it's falling already, 306
But parting is return, the coming home, 145

Come out of the dark earth, 358
Conflict has been our climate for so long, 214
Consider the mysterious salt, 182
Could poetry or love by the same lucky chance, 118
Country of still canals, green willows, golden fields, all, 85
Cried innocence, "Mother, my thumbs, my thumbs, 95

Dear fellow-sufferer, dear cruelty, 203
Dear solid earth after ambiguous seas, 366
Did someone say that there would be an end, 185
Did you achieve this with a simple word, 202

Dorothy Wordsworth, dying, did not want to read, 74

Each branching maple stands in a numb trance, 269
Even in the middle of the silent firs, 354
Even such fervor must seek out an end, 144

Fiery, the tender child, 287
Finite, exact, the square, 56
Fire is a good companion for the mind, 211
First that beautiful mad exploration, 151
For a long time they merely left it there, 292
For a long time, we shall have only to listen, 319
For a time it is part of the machinery, 198
For all the loving words and difficult, 206
For some months now I have lived, 391
For steadfast flame wood must be seasoned, 389
For ten years I have been rooted in these hills, 361
Four years ago I met your death here, 153
France like the map of tenderness fell open, 123
From the rock and from the deep, 263

Great one, austere, 31

Happy the man who can long roaming reap, 265
Have we managed to fade them out like God, 317
Have you not wounded yourself, 379
Having sent memory to prowl, 278
He angled the bright shield, 299
He was there in my room, 130
Heavy, heavy the summer and its gloom, 64
Her name is Kyoko, 227
Here are the peaceful days we never knew, 147

Here in New England where the ice still grips, 392
Here in the olive grove, 173
Here in two ways perspective leads us on, 184
Here is a glass of water from my well, 307
Here is the ample place, 174
Here is the pond, here sky, and the long grasses, 393
Here space, time, peace are given a habitation, 83
Here the traveler, 234
Here where nothing passes, 170
High in Nepal, the lock sprang at last, 250
How little I knew you, Mark, to mourn so wild, 315
How much you have endured of storm, 335
How pure the hearts of lovers as they walk, 141
How sad the thatch, 230
How to lay down her death, 177

I am only beginning to know what I was taught, 63
I am the unicorn and bow my head, 78
I come back from the belly of the whale, 350
I drove home through the morning, rich and still, 372
I found her, rich loser of all, 297
I, in my winter poverty, alone, 409
I looked behind you for the towers of music, 61
I move through my world like a stranger, 163
I moved into my house one day, 210
I never saw my father old, 159
I never thought that it could be, not once, 386
I ponder it again and know for sure, 387
I recognize the quiet and the charm, 337
I saw the world in your face, 79
I saw you once, Medusa; we were alone, 332
I shall not see the end of this unweaving, 201

I think this was a dream, and yet we saw, 101

I thought of happiness, how it is woven, 66

I too have known the inward disturbance of exile, 124

I wake to gentle mist over the meadow, 385

I watched the turtle dwindle day by day, 286

I will lie here alone and live your griefs, 110

I wouldn't know how rare they come these days, 295

If I can let you go as trees let go, 385

If the house is clean and pure, 103

If the one certainty is suffering, 127

If you deny, 107

In early spring, so much like a late autumn, 213

In round straw hats, 231

In space in time I sit, 54

In Texas the lid blew off the sky a long time ago, 50

In the chill dark, 231

In the clean, anodyne, 254

In the end it is the dark for which all lovers pine, 34

In the evening we came back, 136

In the fifth grade, 251

In the late afternoon sun, 247

In the private hour of night, 108

In the snow light, 374

In the West of the country where I was, 313

In this land, Rilke's country if you will, 175

In this suspense of ours before the fall, 347

Indeed I loved these hands and knew them well—, 192

Innocence is the children's country, these, 150

Islands as clouds, 232

It does not mean that we shall find the place, 205

It is autumn again and our anxiety grows, 112

It is contagious as a dance, 284

It is not so much trying to keep alive, 397

It is not what they intend, 402

It is the light, of course, and its great ways, 217

It is time I came back to my real life, 81

It is time the big bird with the angry neck, 181

It was late in September when you took me, 165

James, it is snowing here. It is November, 42

Kind kinderpark, 339

Kyrie Eleison, O wild lynx, 352

Landing, 243

Lately I have been thinking much of those, 334

Let us forget the principalities, 128

Locked to each other's heart, floating at rest, 194

Lovers of water and light, 249

Measure force of tension, 188

My eyes are full of rivers and trees tonight, 67

My parrot is emerald green, 341

My woods belong to woodcock and to deer, 309

Neighbors have come to mow my ragged field, 276

Never forget this when the talk is clever, 86

Not for nothing, here, 240

Not in the cities, not among fabricated towers, 51

Not to rebel against what pulls us down, 179

Nothing could match the era's dazzling façade, 49

Now frost has broken summer like a glass, 218

Now I am coming toward you silently, 80

Now I become myself. It's taken, 156

Now, in the brilliant sun, 375

Now it is Mozart who comes back, 370

Now let us honor with violin and flute, 70

Now silence, silence, silence, and within it, 208

Now that the evening gathers up the day, 144

Now the long lucid listening is done, 289

Now these two warring halves are to be parted, 201

Now voyager, lay here your dazzled head, 73

Now we are balanced, 376

Now we have lost the heartways and the word, 203

Now we must kill or perish, desolate choice—, 91

O cruel cloudless space, 183

O have you heard it, far off, the deep drum, 58

O traveler, tell, what marvels did you see, 260

On a winter night, 155

One death's true death, and that is—not to care, 201

One is large and lazy, 162

Others have cherished, perhaps loved me more, 205

Out of the huge stone fortress, 246

Outside, an April snow, 268

Outside the wind tears at the trees, 105

Pain can make a whole winter bright, 149

Perhaps there is no smallest consolation, 348

Permit the eye so long lost in the inward night, 37

Plain grandeur escapes definition. You, 52

Renewal cannot be picked, 398

Return to the most human, nothing less, 60

"Set the table and sweep the floor—, 365

She did not cry out, 20

She keeps her clavichord, 69

Sheltered under thick thatch, 226

So drive back hating Love and loving Hate, 204

So to release the soul, search out the soul, 144

Sometimes it seems to be the inmost land, 164

Steel gray peaks, 229

Straining the dark, 133

Stretched across counties, countries, the train, 122

Strip off kindness, 168

Summer is all a green air—, 117

Sweet night nursing a neighbor—, 324

Thank God for honesty and anger, 104

That summer, 272

The cat sleeps on my desk in the pale sun, 207

The death of this poet hurts us terribly, 399

"The dragon's Proteus. He must be fought, 187

The evenings are spun glass these winter days, 41

The extreme delicacy of this Easter morning, 351

The fresh sweetness, 230

The frog, that naked creature, 180

The great carp, 232

The great Toby is dead, 169

The house in winter creaks like a ship, 267

The lady said to her lover, 100

The letters ask, 244

The lovely slanting rain, 230

The marriage of this horizontal land, 338

The memory of swans comes back to you in sleep, 36

The old man who had dug the small pit, 394

The old tree peony I had almost given up, 371

The phoebe sits on her nest, 355

The ragged, rough, continental spaces, 244

The rose has opened and is all accomplished, 145

The shadows are all black, 121

The site echoes, 258

The stone withstands, but the chisel destroys, 146

The strangely radiant skies have come, 304
The teacher of logic said, "Reason," 161
The temple stood, holy and perfect, 99
The war games are over, 323
The well drillers, 274
The white walls of this airy house assume, 215
The zinnias, ocher, orange, chrome and amber, 119
There are times when, 316
There by the waterfall, 109
There had been no such music here until, 331
There have been two strangers, 27
There is anxiety hot in the throat, 197
These bulbs forgotten in a cellar, 400
These dormant seas are lifted by the sun, 143
These images remain, these classic landscapes, 146
These nights when the frog grates shrilly by the pond, 63
These riches burst from every barren tree, 208
These were her nightly journeys made alone, 171
They come, expectant, as to a minor Heaven, 285
They make me wince, such vivid dreams rise up, 308
They were intense people, given to migraine, 328
Think, weep, love, O watch, 71
This fullness that is emptiness, 190
This is an ancient scene: we stand and stare, 186
This is the first soft snow, 19
This is the love I bring, 138
This is the time to speak to those who will come after, 39
This landscape does not speak, 55
This lazy prince of tennis balls and lutes, 88
This legendary house, this dear enchanted tomb, 47
This was our testing year after the first, 388
This wind, corruption in the city, 33
Though in a little while, 115

Though we dream of an airy intimacy, 266
Time beats like a heart; we do not hear it, 131
To contemplate this human wisdom, 409
Tonight we come to praise, 333
True gardeners cannot bear a glove, 271
Tumult as deep and formal as in dance, 408
Twice I have set my heart upon a sharing, 387

Under the green leaf hangs a little pouch, 343
Under the leaves an infant love lies dead, 385
Under the wave it is altogether still, 367

Vision is locked in stone, 57

Walking on this dark day through the bewildering city, 40
Was it a long journey for you to begin, 132
We are suddenly there, 189
We are true lovers without hope, 196
We ask the peace of the spirit for each other, 126
We came to Chartres, riding the green plain, 90
We enter this evening as we enter a quartet, 106
We have been struck by a lightning force, 321
We have come back to the cold North, 176
We have seen how dignity can be torn, 344
We have seen the wind and we need not be warned, 84
We have walked, looking at the actual trees, 139
We hold it in our keeping, even apart, 384
We look out, dazzled, at a shining lake, 373
We reach the area of no more hiding, 368
We regretted the rain, 229

We sat smoking at a table by the river, 38

We saw the rich leaves turning brown, 140

We watched the waterfalls, rich and baroque, 388

What angel can I leave, gentle and stern, 146

"What are ruins to us, 257

What if a homing pigeon lost its home, 204

What is experience, O who can tell, 68

What is left at the end, 191

What price serenity these cruel days, 202

What shall we give The Child this day, 96

What soothes the angry snail, 342

What the child saw with dazzled eyes, 381

Whatever find its place now in this edifice, 32

Whatever we found in that room was not easy, 329

When I landed it was coming home, 82

When twilight comes, before it gets too late, 336

When world is reduced, 238

"When you come, 236

Where do I go? Nowhere. And am I, 208

Where once the Moghul princes, 248

Where waterfalls in shining folds, 152

Who could tire of the long shadows, 390

Who wakes now who lay blind with sleep, 89

Why did the woman want to kill one dog, 280

Wild seas, wild seas, and the gulls veering close, 206

Wind in the stiff green wheat, 142

Without the violence, the major shift, 148

Yes, I have been lonely, angry here, 62

You cannot go back now to that innocence—, 35

You cannot see them from the road: go far and deep, 48

You spoke of spring and summer, 53

You thought it heartless, 395

Your greatness withers when it shuts out grief, 203